Contemporary
COOKING

Volume 4

Contemporary
COOKING

Volume 4

3M

Contemporary Cooking

**Editorial production by James Charlton Associates, Ltd.
New York. Editor-in-Chief, James Charlton; Managing
Editors, Barbara Binswanger, Jennie McGregor; Food
Editors, Inez M. Krech, Cecile Lamalle, Anne Lanigan,
Maria Robbins.**

**Book production and manufacturing consulting by:
Cobb/Dunlop Publishing Services, Inc., New York
Art Direction and interior design by:
Marsha Cohen/Parallelogram
Cover design by: Koechel/Peterson Design, Minneapolis**

**Acknowledgments: Allan Baillie, Pat Cocklin, Delu PAL
International, Aire deZanger, Alan Duns, John Elliott, Gus
Francisco, Melvin Grey, Gina Harris, Anthony Kay, Paul
Kemp, David Levin, David Meldrum, Roger Phillips, Nick
Powell, Iain Reid, John Turner, Paul Williams,
George Wright, Cuisinarts, Inc.**

Printed and bound in Yugoslavia by CGP Delo.

Library of Congress Cataloging in Publication Data
Main entry under title:

Contemporary Cooking.

Includes index.
1. Cookery. I. Minnesota Mining and Manufacturing
Company.
TX715.C7586   1984   641.5   84-2563
0-88159-500-4   —   (set)
ISBN: 0-88159-003-7

CONTENTS
for the Contemporary Cooking Series
VOLUME 4

Part One

EGG COOKERY I

Eggs have been an important part of the world's diet from the beginning of history. Long before the chicken was domesticated and confined to the barnyard, people sought out and raided the nests of every sort of bird. Imagine the happiness of the man, woman or child who, having survived the deprivations of a long and dreary winter, subsisting on a monotonous diet of dried and salted food, goes out one fine spring day and finds a nestful of fresh, wholesome eggs. No wonder then that the finding of eggs has always been identified with riches.

They are in fact a treasure, and when hens are allowed to roam free they deposit these treasures in unexpected places. The customs of the egg hunt and the treasure hunt are thus merged. Although relatively few families keep their own chickens today, the ritual persists in yearly Easter egg hunts.

The egg, a miracle of form and function, has been called a nearly perfect food, and in addition, throughout recorded time, it has been endowed with mystical and religious significance.

It poses as an enigma and confronts us with its age-old question: which came first, the chicken or the egg? Which, in turn, perhaps prompted Samuel Butler's famous remark that a hen is only an egg's way of making another egg.

The creation myths of many civilizations have the world beginning as an egg. Out of the great void, say the Hindus, appeared the cosmic egg. It broke into two parts—one silver, one gold. The golden half became the sky, the silver formed the earth below.

In the Finnish epic, *Kalevala,* the world emerges from a broken egg. The golden yolk becomes the sun, the egg whites make the moon, and the eggshell fragments turn into the stars.

In the mythologies of China, Egypt, Persia, and in many legends of native American tribes, the egg plays a prominent role in the creation of the universe.

Eggs represent not only the origins of life, as in the birth of the world, but every year, appearing as they do in springtime, with the increase of light and warmth, they represent rebirth, fertility and all new life. Long before the advent of Christianity, eggs had a place in festivals that celebrated the coming of spring. The word "Easter" comes from *Eostre,* a pagan goddess of spring, whose festival was celebrated in April.

All sorts of rituals and magical beliefs have been associated with eggs. In the early imperial days in Rome, Livia was advised that if she incubated an egg in her bosom she would be able to foretell the sex of her coming baby. According to Pliny, a male chick was hatched and, amazingly enough, Livia gave birth to a son. For a time, it became quite fashionable for pregnant Roman ladies to try to hatch an egg between their breasts.

In Europe, peasants invoked the magical fertility of eggs by using them to smear their plow blades before breaking ground. A young bride in France would ceremonially break an egg upon arriving in her new home, in order to insure fertility.

Brancusi called the egg "the most perfect form in creation," and it is said that when he gave up sculpting it was in despair of ever achieving anything like the perfection of the egg. The egg has been colored, dyed, decorated, painted and bejeweled from time immemorial by almost every culture.

As early as 5000 B.C. eggs were colored red to represent the life force and given as tokens of love and friendship during festivals celebrating the spring equinox.

In China eggs, also dyed red, were given as birthday presents; all over the Middle East colored eggs have always been popular symbolic gifts.

The decorated Easter egg is the most popular form of folk art in the Christian world today. Brilliantly colored eggs, glowing in solid colors or decorated in elaborate and intricate designs, still celebrate the happy springtime of the year.

Perhaps the most famous of all painted Easter eggs are those created by Ukrainian folk artists and called *pysanki.* And although archaeologists have found evidence that the art of painting eggs predates Christianity by thousands of years in the Ukraine, the techniques that are used have remained essentially the same. Elaborate designs are traced in beeswax on the eggshell and the eggs are then dipped repeatedly into vegetable dyes to achieve the desired brilliant colors. The designs themselves are based on elements from nature— the sun, stars, flowers, etc.

Regardless of holidays or seasons, eggs are the basis of an enormous variety of delicious and popular dishes all year round. Although in the United States eggs are all too often relegated to the breakfast menu, in most other countries eggs are more commonly eaten as part of a lunch or dinner. In Ancient Greece, eggs were considered a suitable ending to a lavish meal; they were served along with nuts and pastries for dessert. Louis XIV made a habit of eating several hard-cooked eggs after dessert and entertained his courtiers with his skill at slicing off the tops with a single quick stroke.

A hard-cooked egg dish called *beid* is quite popular in the Middle East. The eggs are colored yellow or brown, then flavored with cuminseed, coriander or cinnamon. They are sold as snacks by street vendors and are accompanied by a rolled-up paper cone that holds the seasonings to dip them in.

Indeed, eggs cooked in the shell have been popular for a very long time. It is thought that Queen Victoria introduced the custom of eating them at breakfast, using a golden eggcup and a little golden spoon.

In *A Little Tour of France,* Henry James immortalized the eggs he ate at Bourg. "I walked back into town from the church . . . and as the hour of the midday breakfast had struck, directed my steps to the inn. The table d'hôte was going on, and a gracious, bustling, talkative landlady welcomed me. I had an excellent repast—the best repast possible—which consisted simply of boiled eggs and bread and butter. It was the quality of these simple ingredients that made the occasion so memorable. The eggs were so good that I am ashamed to say how many of them I consumed."

There are many jokes about the inexperienced cook who can't even boil an egg, but a good cook never boils an egg, only just simmers it. Boiling water gives eggs a rubbery texture, and bumping around in the pan is liable to crack the shells so that strands of egg escape and the insides get soggy.

Gentle heat is also essential for making perfect poached eggs as well as light, creamy scrambled eggs.

"They know in France 685 different ways of dressing eggs," wrote Grimod de la Reynière, and if you add to that number the many ways with eggs of other countries, then we can truly substantiate the claim that there is no single food more versatile than the egg.

The hard-cooked egg is as welcome in the picnic basket as it is in the most sumptuous buffet. It is an essential ingredient in an enormous number of cocktail snacks, canapés, sandwiches and salads. It can be cut into halves, with the yolks removed and turned into a savory paste which is then heaped back into the perfect white container to make that most popular of party foods—stuffed eggs.

Eggs can be scrambled on their own with butter and a little cream or can incorporate a stunning variety of other ingredients to make elegant and delicious dishes to serve at almost any meal.

While a poached egg is a lovely thing served on its own with simple buttered toast, it too becomes the basis of many luxuriously sauced and elegant main course dishes.

A riddle, posed by Tolkien in *The Hobbit,* aptly describes the miracle that is the egg: "A box without hinges, key or lid,/Yet golden treasure inside is hid."

EGGS

Freshness. For the most part we have little choice when purchasing eggs and are dependent on what is available in the market. Supermarket eggs are usually of reliable quality as they have been stored in optimum conditions. While it is unlikely that you will get an egg that is only a day or so old, neither will you find a rotten one.

Should you find yourself in the country with access to newly laid eggs, here are a few things you should know: The very freshest eggs are ideal for poaching. With no trouble on your part you will have a perfectly poached egg with no ragged edges and tough stringy parts. The older the eggs, the more trouble it will be to poach them perfectly.

On the other hand, if perfectly peeled hard-cooked eggs are important, eggs that are too fresh will not perform as you want them to. If you know your eggs are very fresh and you want to be able to peel them after they are cooked, leave them out of the refrigerator, uncovered, for a day or two.

Color. Contrary to popular belief, brown eggs are not any better for you than white ones. In terms of taste and nutritional value they are exactly the same, although they will often cost more. The color of the shell is simply an indication of the breed of hen that laid it. There are hens that lay eggs bluish-green in color, but since these are not used in the mass production of eggs, you will not find them on the supermarket shelf.

The color of the yolk has nothing to do with nutritional value or the freshness of the egg; it depends entirely on the diet of the hen.

Size and Grade. Commercial egg production is a finely mechanized science. Eggs are sized by their weight per dozen. Jumbo eggs must weigh 30 ounces or more; Extra Large between 27 and 30 ounces; Large between 24 and 27 ounces; Medium between 21 and 24 ounces; Small between 18 and 21 ounces.

Eggs are also graded according to their freshness: Grade AA (Fancy Fresh) being the freshest, on down through A, B and C.

Storing Eggs. An egg contains an air space, which gradually expands as the egg loses its freshness. Quality is better maintained if this air space is kept floating at the broad end of the egg; therefore always store an egg with the pointed end down.

Eggshells are porous, so keep them in a covered container and store them well away from strong-smelling foods.

Light destroys the keeping quality and vitamin content, so eggs should be stored in a cool dark place. A refrigerator provides ideal long-term storage for eggs, but they will keep in a cool larder for several weeks.

Refrigerated eggs should be brought to room temperature before placing them in boiling water, so as not to crack the shells.

Eggs Cooked in the Shells

The most important thing to know about an egg perfectly cooked in the shell is that the egg must never *boil*, but only *simmer*. The excess heat and violent agitation caused by boiling water makes an egg tough and causes a dark line between the yolk and the white.

Cooking the Eggs

Equipment. Reserve a small deep pan with a well-fitting lid specifically for cooking eggs in the shell. An inexpensive enamel pan is ideal.

Use a tablespoon, perforated draining spoon, wire basket or egg holder to lift eggs safely in and out of the water. A holder or basket allows several eggs to be lowered into the water at once, which makes timing less complicated.

Piercing the blunt end before immersing an egg in water is another precaution against cracking the shell during cooking. An optional but useful tool is an egg prick—a small gadget which releases a needle point when pressed. Or use a pin.

Accurate timing equipment is vital. Egg timers are traditional but an oven clock or a watch with a second hand makes precise timing easier.

Method 1: Bring enough water to a boil to cover the eggs by at least 1 inch, and lower the heat immediately so that the water barely simmers. Gently lower eggs into the water and begin timing.

Method 2: Place eggs in cold water to cover. Bring to the boil and reduce heat to a simmer. Begin timing when water comes to the boil.

Timing. The time needed to cook an egg to perfection depends partly on personal taste (see chart). A very fresh egg cooks more slowly than one that is several days old.

Minutes to cook eggs in the shell
(Large, Medium, Small)

Method 1	L	M	S
Very soft-cooked (yolk runny, white soft)	4	3½	3
Soft-cooked (yolk soft, white firm)	5	4½	4
Hard-cooked (yolk and white very firm)	11	10½	10
Method 2	L	M	S
Very soft-cooked	3	2½	2
Soft-cooked	4	3½	3
Hard-cooked	8	7	6

Peeling Eggs. Eggs continue cooking even after they have been removed from the pan, so the cooking process must be arrested as soon as the time is up. Either plunge the eggs into cold water or, in the case of a breakfast egg, lightly tap with a spoon

Eggs Cooked in the Shell

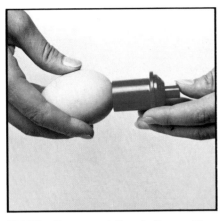

1 To prevent the shells cracking, use eggs at room temperature and if desired, pierce the round ends.

2 Bring water to boiling point. Lower the eggs on a spoon into the water. Immediately reduce the heat to a simmer, cover the pan, and start timing.

OR Place eggs in a single layer in a pan. Add enough cold water to cover them. Cover the pan and bring to boil. Reduce to a simmer and start timing.

3 To center the yolks in hard-cooked eggs, turn once or twice during the first minute of cooking. Remove the eggs from the pan as soon as the time is up.

4 For breakfast eggs, tap the shells to prevent further cooking. For hard-cooked eggs, immediately plunge eggs into cold water. Remove after 1 minute.

5 To peel hard-cooked eggs, gently tap shells all over. Carefully peel away a central band, then slip off ends of shell. Reserve eggs in warm or cold water.

to crack open the crown of the shell. Cold water stops the cooking process and also makes the egg easier to peel because it shrinks the skin and this helps detach the shell. You can insure even easier peeling of hard-cooked eggs by cracking each one gently in 2 or 3 places and returning it to the cold water bath for a few more minutes.

The eggs will be easiest to peel if you allow them to cool completely first. Tap the shell lightly all over until it is broken into tiny fragments. Beginning at the large end, start to peel away membrane and shell. You may do this while holding the egg under running water.

Alternatively, roll the egg on a hard surface, pressing down with the palm of your hand until shell is completely cracked and fragmented. Peel.

Exposing an egg to air toughens it, giving the white an unpleasant rubbery texture, and refrigeration dries out the yolk. So immerse shelled eggs immediately in a bowl of cold water or warm water if the eggs are for a hot dish. Leave until required, then dry carefully with a cloth or paper towel.

Tarragon-Flavored Eggs. Wrap fresh eggs individually in tarragon leaves, then in foil. Leave the eggs in the refrigerator for 24 hours. Next day, soft-cook the eggs in the shells. They will have absorbed the herb flavor through the porous shell, and the

6

finished eggs will be delicately flavored with tarragon.

Other fresh herbs can be used in the same way; strong-flavored herbs are most successful.

Decorating Eggs

Whether you are decorating eggs especially for Easter, or just for the fun of it on a rainy afternoon, it is an agreeable and pleasant occupation for grown-ups and children alike.

Decorated eggs can be as simple or as elaborate as your patience and skill permit. Here are a few basics to get you started:
• Use white eggs.
• Most commercially produced eggs are sprayed with a fine mist of tasteless mineral oil to keep them fresh, but the oil will also prevent dyes from adher-

ing. Wash the eggs carefully with soap and warm water before beginning.
• If you plan to eat the eggs, then hard-cook them before beginning.
• Otherwise, pierce each end of the egg with a pin or egg piercer and blow out the contents; use contents for scrambled eggs.
• Use food coloring or natural dyes extracted from tea, onion skins, beets, etc.

Hard-cooked Egg Garnishes

1 Use a slicer or wedger for very precise cuts, or a stainless-steel knife with a serrated edge.

2 Eggs can be cut into halves lengthwise or across. Slice off the bottom of a half to make it stand level.

3 Use a teaspoon to remove the yolk. Do the job slowly and carefully to avoid breaking the white.

4 For stuffings and garnishes, rub the yolk through a fine sieve. Sieved yolks are called "mimosa."

5 Use a teaspoon or piping bag to fill hollows with stuffing: mashed yolk plus flavorings and liquid.

6 Hold both handle and tip of a sharp knife and chop across eggs without moving blade tip.

Serving Ideas for Hard-Cooked Eggs

There are literally hundreds of ways that hard-cooked eggs can be served. Primarily, they are the ideal snack and picnic food.

Peeled, sliced lengthwise, and garnished with a bit of mayonnaise and a snippet of fresh herbs, they are an appealing beginning to any meal. Any of the following savory toppings may be used to garnish a sliced hard-cooked egg: parsley sprigs, fresh tarragon leaves, fresh dill, pimento strips, anchovies, olives, capers, strips of ham or prosciutto, tiny shrimps, crab meat, sardines.

Stuffed hard-cooked eggs are extremely popular as appetizers, part of a buffet table or included in a picnic basket. To stuff hard-cooked eggs, halve each egg lengthwise and carefully remove the yolk. Cover the hollow whites with plastic wrap so that they do not dry out and discolor. Sieve the yolks into a mixing bowl. All sorts of flavorings can be used for stuffing eggs but the mixture should always be soft but firm. Combine with any of the following: mayonnaise, mustard, vinaigrette, yogurt, sour cream or béchamel. Season to taste with salt and pepper, and flavor with cayenne, curry powder, Worcestershire sauce, Tabasco®. Any number of savory ingredients can be added. Choose from minced scallions, celery, watercress, smoked salmon, caviar, tuna fish, ham or sausage.

Use a teaspoon or a pastry tube to replace the filling in the hollow egg whites. Garnish with fresh herbs, olives, or capers.

Stuffed eggs can be prepared in advance and kept in a cool place. Cover them lightly with foil to prevent drying at the edges if storing in the refrigerator for more than an hour.

The sieved yolks of hard-cooked eggs make an attractive garnish for fresh green salads and steamed green vegetables such as asparagus and broccoli. This type of garnish is called *mimosa.*

Sliced and quartered hard-cooked eggs may be used as a garnish for almost any type of salad and hors d'oeuvre plate.

Hard-cooked eggs can be combined with vegetables and cooked in a variety of casserole dishes that make delicious main courses.

Cracking an Egg

 **1** Crack the shell by giving it a sharp tap across the center on the edge of a cup.

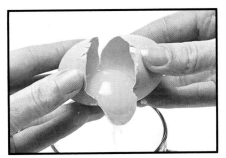 **2** Put your thumbs into the crack and pull the shell apart, then slide the egg gently into the cup.

 **3** If small bits of shell stick to the egg, remove them carefully with a teaspoon.

SCRAMBLED EGGS

Scrambled eggs, cooked to perfection so that they are light as air and evenly creamy throughout, make an elegant dish for a breakfast or a banquet. Anyone can master the few simple rules that will forever banish scrambled eggs that are too wet, stringy or dried out.

Scrambled eggs should always be made with butter; unsalted is best. Nothing else can give them that very special taste, and because butter melts at the same low temperature as eggs cook they can be stirred together over very low heat for a creamy texture. The exception is in dishes such as pipérade where oil is used in place of butter to cook the vegetables, to which eggs are added.

Equipment. A heavy pan with a nonstick surface is ideal. A wooden spoon for stirring; a mixing bowl and fork.

There are 2 golden rules to perfect scrambled eggs:

1 Never use anything other than butter, cream or milk to thin or enrich the egg mixture, otherwise the results will be weak and watery.
2 Moderately low heat is essential. Too much heat makes the eggs dry and rubbery. Move the pan away

8

from the heat if the mixture is scrambling too fast.

If serving the scrambled eggs hot, have the diners ready-seated and waiting: perfection in scrambled eggs does not last long.

If the scrambled eggs are to be served cold, turn them into a cold bowl as soon as they are cooked to arrest

further cooking, and cover the bowl until required. Don't make the scrambled eggs too far ahead, as the mixture will congeal or may separate. Never leave scrambled eggs in the pan to cool.

It is commonplace (and more economical) to use whole eggs, but for a really smooth texture, professional cooks use 1 extra yolk to every 3 whole

eggs. This gives the finished dish a beautiful golden color as well as improving the texture, and is worth remembering for special occasions.

The eggs are broken into a bowl, lightly beaten with a fork to amalgamate the whites and yolks, and seasoned. Butter is heated in the pan until just melted and the eggs are poured in and cooked over moderately low heat. Stir

Scrambled Eggs

4 portions

6   large eggs
2   extra egg yolks
    salt and black pepper
4   tablespoons butter or 2
        tablespoons butter and 2
        tablespoons thick cream

1 Break eggs into a bowl; add yolks and salt and pepper to taste. Beat lightly with fork to blend whites and yolks.

2 Melt 2 tablespoons of the butter in a heavy pan over low heat, making sure it does not get too hot.

4 As mixture starts to thicken, stir more rapidly, particularly around pan base and sides.

5 Just before mixture reaches the right consistency, remove pan from heat. Keep on stirring.

6 As soon as the right texture is reached, add the rest of the butter or the cream and stir in.

slowly but continuously with a wooden spoon, taking care to reach all the bottom surface of the pan so that the eggs cook evenly.

Nothing appears to happen for the first 2 or 3 minutes as the eggs are warming up. Then suddenly they begin to thicken, so start stirring more rapidly. Remember that eggs continue cooking even after they have been taken off the heat, so remove the pan from the stove just before they reach the desired consistency.

Keep stirring, and as soon as the right texture is reached, stir in more butter or thick cream. This will enrich the eggs and, because it is cold, effectively arrests cooking. Use butter at room temperature, and do not use more than the specified amount of cream as too much might cause separation.

3 Pour eggs into the melted butter and stir slowly with a wooden spoon for 2 to 3 minutes.

7 Serve immediately on hot buttered toast. Garnish with chopped fresh parsley or snipped chives.

Serving Ideas for Scrambled Eggs

Any of the following can be added to the basic scrambled egg recipe. For hot scrambled eggs, make sure that additional cooked ingredients are also hot when you add them.

• Add 1 to 2 tablespoons of minced or snipped fresh parsley, chives, chervil or tarragon to the eggs, either before or during cooking.

• Wash and slice 6 to 8 mushrooms and cook them gently in 2 tablespoons of butter. Add to the scrambled eggs after the cream. Reserve a few mushroom slices for garnishing.

• Add 8 to 10 small shrimps, cooked and shelled, to the eggs after the cream. Reserve one or two for garnish.

• Add 2 ounces Gruyère or other cheese, grated, to the eggs at the enrichment stage. Garnish with parsley sprigs or snipped chives.

• Cut 2 to 4 ounces of ham into strips, heat in a little butter, and add to the eggs at the enrichment stage. Garnish with snipped chives or scallion tops.

• Incorporate 2 to 4 ounces of smoked salmon, cut into thin strips, adding a little lemon juice to the salmon when heating it. Add to the eggs at the enrichment stage.

• Add 2 chicken livers, sautéed and chopped, or 4 strips of bacon, cooked crisp and crumbled, to the eggs after the cream. Garnish with chopped fresh parsley.

POACHED EGGS

A plump, compact, perfectly poached egg is one of the loveliest dishes imaginable. It makes an ideal breakfast on its own with a piece of good toast, or it can become the basis or garnish of many delicious and versatile dishes.

Equipment. Choose a wide pan that allows the depth of the water to be 2 to 3 inches; the sides of the pan should be low enough to allow you to handle the eggs easily.

To roll the eggs and lift them out of the water you need a perforated metal spoon.

Other equipment includes a cup or saucer to break the eggs into, absorbent kitchen paper to remove the moisture, kitchen scissors to trim the whites and, if you are not serving the eggs immediately, a bowl of cold or warm water in which to keep them until use.

The lidded pans with hollow spaces and "saucers" that are sold as egg poachers do not really poach eggs at all. They steam them, making the whites hard and leathery. For this reason eggs cooked in them cannot be truly termed poached.

Poached eggs are usually cooked in gently simmering water with a few drops of vinegar added to help the white coagulate and hold its shape. But milk, stock or wine can be used instead for special occasions.

Poaching Eggs. To cook a perfectly poached egg you need a little practice, but the method explained here will give very good results.

Although it is possible to poach 3 or 4 eggs simultaneously, it is wiser to poach only one at a time until you feel you have perfected the technique.

Poached Eggs

1 Heat 2 to 3 inches of water in a wide pan and add a few drops of vinegar. Break egg into a saucer.

2 When the water is simmering, stir it around quickly with a spoon to make a whirlpool.

3 Holding the saucer close to the liquid, slip the egg into the center of the whirlpool.

4 As water becomes still, roll egg over with a perforated spoon to distribute white evenly around yolk.

5 Cook for 3½ to 4 minutes, then take the egg out of the water with a perforated spoon.

6 Blot with absorbent kitchen paper to remove moisture, and trim with kitchen scissors if necessary.

Use fresh eggs at room temperature. Heat 2 to 3 inches of water in a wide pan and add a few drops of vinegar. Break each egg into a saucer or cup. When the water is simmering, stir it round into a whirlpool and, holding the saucer as close to the liquid as possible, slip the egg into the pan. As soon as the water is no longer swirling (it should be barely simmering), roll the egg over with a perforated spoon so as to push the white around the yolk. The egg should be perfectly cooked in 3½ to 4 minutes.

Lift it out carefully with the perforated spoon. Flip it over onto absorbent kitchen towels to remove any moisture and from there onto hot buttered toast or a serving dish. If necessary you can cut away any ragged edges with kitchen scissors.

It is not absolutely necessary to make a whirlpool, though it does help to keep the egg together. You can slip the egg into barely simmering water which is not swirling; without a whirlpool it is easier to poach more than 1 egg at a time. In this case add each

additional egg to the water 2 to 3 seconds after rolling the previous one over, and so on. It is important to make sure the water is only just simmering and that there is as little movement in the water as possible.

If you are nervous that the eggs will not keep their shape or that they are not quite as fresh as you would wish, you can place them in their shells in a wire basket or sieve and immerse them in simmering water for 10 to 15 seconds. This will firm up the whites just enough to hold them in shape around the yolks. Then break each egg into a saucer and poach as described.

Keeping and Reheating. Poached eggs can be cooked several hours in advance, but should be kept in cold water so that they stay supple and do not become leathery.

To reheat them, put them into freshly heated hand-hot water and leave for a few minutes to warm through.

Serving Ideas for Poached Eggs

Once you have mastered the art of poaching and your eggs are well rounded with a soft yolk inside a film of white, the different ways in which they can be served will soon convince you that the little patience it takes to make them is really worthwhile.

• For a traditional breakfast, serve poached eggs on hot buttered toast, with bacon or sausages.

• Serve them with a mushroom topping on hot buttered toast, or in boat-shaped tartlet cases. Use 4 to 6 small mushrooms, 1 tablespoon butter and 2 tablespoons thin cream per egg. Slice the mushrooms and cook them gently in the butter. Add a pinch of cayenne pepper. Stir in the cream, spoon mushrooms over the egg and serve. Remember to blot the egg, otherwise the sauce will slide off the wet surface.

• For a lunch or supper dish, serve poached eggs on top of creamy mashed potatoes topped with Mornay sauce. Sprinkle with cheese and place briefly under a hot broiler to melt and brown the cheese.

• Poached eggs in baked potatoes make a good light lunch. Cut the top off the hot potato, scoop out a third of the inside, and drop in a knob of butter.

Place the poached egg in the hollow, grate a little cheese on top, and serve.

• For masked eggs, place sliced tomatoes in individual ramekins, put a cold poached egg in each ramekin on top of the tomato, and coat with mayonnaise. Decorate with small pieces of pimiento, olives, chives, etc., to look like flowers.

• For poached eggs Lucullus you will need 8 ounces mushrooms, chopped, and 2 large Boston lettuces, shredded, for 4 people. Sauté the mushrooms and lettuce in 4 tablespoons butter and season well. Turn into a gratin dish. Poach 4 eggs and make an indentation for each in the dish. Sprinkle with grated cheese and brown under the broiler.

• Many people consider *Eggs Benedict* to be the most elegant way to serve poached eggs, and in fact, Hollandaise sauce goes particularly well with poached eggs.

Egg and Bacon Scramble

4 portions

1	medium-size onion
4	small zucchini, about 1 pound altogether
2	large tomatoes
4	ounces button mushrooms
8	slices of smoked bacon
1	tablespoon vegetable oil
½	teaspoon salt
¼	teaspoon black pepper
6	eggs
¼	cup milk
⅛	teaspoon grated nutmeg
1	cup fresh white bread crumbs
1	tablespoon butter

Peel and mince the onion. Wash and trim zucchini and chop them. Blanch and peel the tomatoes, and chop them. Trim the stems of the mushrooms, wipe mushrooms with a damp cloth, and cut each button into halves through cap and stem. Chop the bacon.

Heat the oil in a shallow flameproof casserole over moderate heat. When oil is hot, add onion and bacon and cook, stirring occasionally, for 7 minutes, until onion is soft but not brown and bacon is cooked. Add zucchini, tomatoes, mushrooms, salt and pepper. Reduce heat to low and cook, stirring occasionally, for 15 minutes, until vegetables are tender and well mixed. Remove casserole from heat. Preheat broiler to high.

Break the eggs into a mixing bowl. Add milk and nutmeg and beat together. Stir the mixture into the casserole of vegetables. Return casserole to heat and cook gently, stirring constantly, until the eggs are nearly scrambled. Remove casserole from heat. Sprinkle the bread crumbs on top of the mixture. Cut the butter into tiny bits and scatter on the bread crumbs. Place the casserole under the broiler for 3 minutes, until the top is lightly browned. Serve at once.

Soft-Cooked Eggs with Spinach and Tomatoes

4 portions

8 soft-cooked eggs	4 ounces cooked ham
4 tablespoons unsalted butter	salt and pepper
	grated nutmeg
1 pound fresh spinach, or 10 ounces frozen chopped spinach	4 ounces Cheddar cheese, grated (1 cup)
4 medium-size tomatoes	2 tablespoons grated Parmesan cheese

Carefully shell the eggs, keeping them whole, and gently lower them into a bowl of warm water. Preheat oven to 250°F. Use 1 tablespoon of the butter to coat the bottom and sides of a large gratin dish.

Cook the fresh spinach in boiling salted water for 5 minutes. Drain, rinse with cold water, and drain again. Chop the spinach in the colander and let it drain until ready to use. If the spinach is frozen, cook according to package directions and drain well. Cut the tomatoes into thin slices and the ham into 3-inch strips. Arrange the tomato slices in the gratin dish and scatter the ham strips on top.

Melt remaining butter over low heat. Stir in the well-drained spinach until it is buttery and hot. Season generously with salt, pepper and nutmeg. Spread the spinach over the ham and tomatoes and make 8 small indentations in it with the back of a tablespoon. Cover the dish with foil and keep warm in the low oven.

Drain the eggs and pat them dry. Remove the foil from the gratin dish from the oven and preheat the broiler. Place 1 egg in each indentation in the spinach. Sprinkle the Cheddar cheese over the eggs and the Parmesan cheese on top. Put the dish under the broiler and broil until the cheese topping has melted and turned golden and bubbling.

Eggs with Tarragon Mayonnaise

4 portions

1 cup mayonnaise	1½ tablespoons boiling water
1 tablespoon tarragon vinegar	6 hard-cooked eggs
1 teaspoon minced fresh tarragon, or ¼ teaspoon dried	12 lettuce leaves
	4 flat anchovy fillets
1 teaspoon snipped fresh chives	1 tablespoon chopped parsley

In a mixing bowl combine the mayonnaise, tarragon vinegar, minced fresh tarragon and snipped chives. Add the boiling water, 1 teaspoon at a time, until the mayonnaise has a good coating consistency. Taste, and add seasoning or more tarragon vinegar if necessary.

Shell the eggs and halve them lengthwise. Wash and dry the lettuce leaves and divide them among 4 salad plates. Place 3 egg halves, cut sides down, arranged like a 3-petaled flower, on the lettuce on each plate. Coat the eggs with a thin layer of mayonnaise. Curl 1 anchovy fillet to make a center for each flower. Sprinkle the top with parsley and serve.

Eggs Stuffed with Herbs

4 portions

4 hard-cooked eggs fresh herbs: parsley, chives, dill	2 tablespoons heavy cream salt and pepper 1 bunch of watercress

Shell the eggs, halve them lengthwise, and scoop out the yolks. Rub the yolks through a fine sieve into a bowl. Remove parsley stems and mince the leaves. Snip chives and dill sprigs. The proportions can be adjusted to your taste, but mince and snip enough to have 4 teaspoons altogether. Add herbs and cream to the sieved yolks and season with salt and pepper. Mix thoroughly with a wooden spoon and check the seasoning again.

Use a teaspoon to mound the yolk mixture in the whites; or pipe out the stuffing with a pastry bag fitted with a star nozzle. Wash and dry the watercress sprigs. Arrange the eggs on a bed of watercress.

Variations: Instead of herbs, use 3 tablespoons smoked fish roe pounded to a paste with a little olive oil, lemon juice and puréed garlic. Or use 3 tablespoons minced lean ham with a little chopped scallion and a dash of Worcestershire sauce. Or skin and bone 2 large sardines and mash to a smooth paste with lemon juice. Or mix the yolks with 1½ tablespoons Dijon-style mustard and a little grated fresh horseradish or chopped capers.

Mexican Stuffed Eggs

6 portions

6	hard-cooked eggs
1	medium-size ripe avocado
1	small onion
1	small green pepper
4	ounces cooked crab meat or lobster meat
1	teaspoon lemon juice
1	teaspoon wine vinegar
½	teaspoon salt
½	teaspoon black pepper
⅛	teaspoon cayenne pepper
1	tablespoon chopped fresh parsley

Shell the eggs and halve them lengthwise. Press the yolks through a fine sieve into a bowl. Peel the avocado, remove the pit, and push the flesh through the same fine sieve into the yolks. Peel and mince the onion. Wash the pepper, halve it, and discard stem, seeds and ribs; mince the pepper. Flake or chop the crab or lobster, being sure to remove any bits of cartilage. Add onion, pepper and shellfish to the egg yolks. Pour in the lemon juice and vinegar, and add salt, black pepper and cayenne. With a wooden spoon, stir the mixture to combine the ingredients evenly.

Stuff the egg whites with the filling, mounding it up in the center and covering most of the cut surface of the whites. Arrange the eggs on a serving dish and sprinkle them with parsley. Chill the eggs in the refrigerator for 30 minutes before serving as an appetizer or as part of a buffet meal.

Eggs with Shrimps and Cheese

4 portions

8   hard-cooked eggs
1   tablespoon butter
1   tablespoon snipped fresh
     chives
1   teaspoon dried tarragon
1   tablespoon prepared
     Dijon-style mustard

8   ounces small shrimps,
     cooked, shelled and
     deveined
½   teaspoon salt
¼   teaspoon white pepper
1   cup light cream
2   ounces Cheddar cheese,
     grated (½ cup)

Shell the eggs, and chop them. In a saucepan, melt the butter over moderate heat. Add the eggs, chives, tarragon, mustard, shrimps, salt and pepper, and stir to mix. Stir in the cream and heat the mixture for 5 to 6 minutes, until it has thickened slightly.

Preheat the broiler to high. Transfer the egg mixture to a medium-size flameproof dish. Sprinkle the cheese on top. Broil the mixture for 2 to 3 minutes, until the top is lightly browned. Serve at once.

Matzo Brei

(Scrambled Eggs with Matzos)

4 portions

4   large matzos
1   cup milk
4   eggs

½   teaspoon salt
⅛   teaspoon grated nutmeg
2   tablespoons butter

Break the matzos into 2-inch pieces and put them in a bowl. Pour the milk over the pieces and let them soak for about 5 minutes. With a slotted spoon transfer the matzos to another bowl. Discard any leftover milk.

Break the eggs into a bowl and beat lightly. Pour the eggs onto the matzos. Add salt and nutmeg and mix well with a wooden spoon. Melt the butter in a saucepan over moderate heat. When the foam subsides, pour in the matzo and egg mixture. Cook for 5 to 7 minutes, stirring constantly, until the eggs are firm and only slightly moist. Transfer the mixture to a warmed serving dish and serve immediately.

Eggs Stuffed with Caviar

6 portions

6 hard-cooked eggs	1 teaspoon lemon juice
2 tablespoons black or red caviar	¼ teaspoon cayenne pepper

Shell the eggs, halve them lengthwise and scoop out the yolks. Cut a thin slice off the bottom of each half so it will stand level. Press the yolks through a fine sieve into a bowl. With a fork, mix the caviar, lemon juice and cayenne into the yolks. Spoon the mixture into the egg whites and to cover the entire surface. Arrange the eggs in a serving dish and chill in the refrigerator for 30 minutes.

Russian Easter Eggs

To color eggs, natural vegetable dyes or food coloring should be used. Use only white-shelled eggs. Place eggs in a saucepan containing the chosen dye and bring the liquid to a boil. Simmer the eggs over low heat for 10 minutes. Remove pan from heat and lift out the eggs with a slotted spoon. Pat eggs dry with paper towels and set them aside to cool.

If the egg is to remain a plain color, rub it with vegetable oil. If the egg is to be further colored or decorated, rub it with vegetable oil only when it is completely decorated.

Color Guide for Natural Vegetable Dyes

yellow: use the outer skins of onions
red, pink: use raw beets
green: use birch leaves

Boil the ingredient until you have the intensity of color that is desired.

Alternatively, a few drops of edible food coloring can be used; these are available in red, blue, green and yellow.

Decorating the eggs. Onion skins wrapped around the eggs and tied on with cotton thread develop a marble effect when the skins are removed.

Eggs wrapped in pieces of silk and tied with cotton take on a "tie-dye" effect when unwrapped.

Thin strips of masking tape stuck on the eggs in various geometric and flower patterns, before boiling the eggs in dye, will reveal patterns in white when the tape is removed.

Flower petals stuck to damp, uncooked eggs and then covered with onion or shallot skins, tied on with cotton thread, produce flower-patterned yellow eggs.

Dental floss or cotton thread rubbed in paraffin and wound around the eggs, then removed when the eggs are cold, produces a myriad of lined patterns. Unwaxed cotton thread produces deeper-colored patterned lines.

Eggs that are simmered gently in an edible food color may be hand-painted with other edible food colors to any design you choose.

The eggs should be eaten within 48 hours after dyeing and decorating.

Eggs with Gruyère Cheese and Rosemary

4 portions

8 soft-cooked eggs	6 ounces Gruyère cheese, grated (1½ cups)
2 cups béchamel sauce (see Volume 3 index)	1 teaspoon minced fresh rosemary, or ½ teaspoon dried

Preheat the broiler. Carefully shell the eggs, keeping them whole, and place 2 eggs in each of 4 individual ramekins or shirred-egg dishes. Pour the sauce into a saucepan and bring it to a boil over moderate heat, stirring constantly. Reduce heat to the lowest possible and stir in the cheese and rosemary. Cook, stirring frequently, until cheese has melted and sauce is very hot. Pour the sauce over the eggs. Slide the ramekins under the broiler for 2 minutes, until the tops are golden brown. Serve immediately.

Eggs in White-Wine Sauce

4 portions

4 soft-cooked eggs	⅔ cup brown stock
1 medium-size onion	½ teaspoon salt
1 tablespoon butter	½ teaspoon black pepper
1 tablespoon flour	1 tablespoon prepared Dijon-style mustard
⅔ cup white wine	

Shell the eggs, keeping them whole, and place each one in an individual ½-cup baking dish; keep the eggs warm. Peel and mince the onion. Melt the butter in a small saucepan over moderate heat. Add onion to the butter and cook, stirring often, for 5 to 7 minutes, until onion is soft and translucent but not brown. With a wooden spoon stir in the flour to make a smooth paste. Cook, stirring, for 1 minute. Off the heat, gradually stir in the wine and stock, being careful to avoid lumps. Add salt, pepper and mustard. Return pan to heat and simmer the sauce for 5 minutes, stirring often. Divide the sauce among the baking dishes and serve the eggs at once, with buttered toast.

Pipérade Basque

(Scrambled Eggs with Tomatoes, Onions and Peppers)

6 portions

1 onion	1½ pounds tomatoes
1 garlic clove	salt and black pepper
4 medium-size green peppers	pinch of sugar
	pinch of dried basil
1 to 2 tablespoons olive oil	4 eggs

Peel and mince the onion. Peel garlic and put through a press into the onion. Wash peppers, halve them, and remove stems, seeds and ribs. Cut peppers into thick slices. Heat the oil in a large skillet. Cook the onion and garlic over low heat until onion is golden. Add the peppers and cook for about 10 minutes longer. Peel and chop the tomatoes. Add the tomatoes, salt and pepper to taste, the sugar and basil and cook, stirring occasionally, until tomatoes are reduced to a lumpy purée.

Break the eggs into a bowl and beat with a fork until well mixed but not frothy. Pour eggs into the skillet. Cook over gentle heat, stirring with a wooden spoon, to mix the eggs into the sauce. Remove from heat before the eggs are completely cooked, but continue to stir until they are scrambled. Serve immediately.

Scrambled Eggs with Cream and Herbs

4 portions

8 eggs	½ teaspoon salt
¼ cup milk	¼ teaspoon black pepper
3 tablespoons heavy cream	⅛ teaspoon paprika
2 teaspoons snipped fresh chives	1 tablespoon butter
1 teaspoon minced fresh chervil	1 tablespoon minced fresh parsley

Break the eggs into a mixing bowl and beat with a wire whisk or a rotary beater until light and frothy. Beat in the milk, cream, chives, chervil, salt, pepper and paprika. Melt the butter in a heavy saucepan over low heat. When the foam subsides, pour in the egg and herb mixture and cook, stirring constantly with a wooden spoon, until eggs are lightly scrambled. Turn the mixture into a warmed serving dish, sprinkle parsley on top, and serve immediately.

Ricotta and Olive Scramble

4 portions

1	cup pitted green olives	¼	cup milk
1	red bell pepper	½	teaspoon black pepper
4	ounces ricotta cheese	½	teaspoon dried basil
3	tablespoons olive oil	2	ounces Parmesan cheese, grated (½ cup)
6	eggs		

Rinse the olives to remove excess brine. Cut olives into quarters, or chop them roughly. Wash the pepper, halve it, and remove stem, seeds and ribs; chop the pepper. With a fork, break up the ricotta cheese. Preheat broiler to high.

Heat the olive oil in a shallow flameproof casserole over moderate heat. When oil is hot, add the olives and red pepper and cook, stirring frequently, for 3 minutes. Add the ricotta and cook over low heat, stirring constantly, for 2 minutes longer.

Break the eggs into a bowl and add the milk, pepper and basil. Beat together until mixed. Reduce heat under the casserole to very low and pour in the egg mixture. Cook, stirring constantly, until eggs are nearly scrambled. Remove casserole from heat. Sprinkle the Parmesan cheese on top of the eggs and slide the casserole under the broiler for 3 minutes, until the cheese has melted and the top is lightly browned. Serve at once.

Basque Eggs with Artichokes

4 portions

4	cooked large artichoke bottoms, fresh or canned
1	onion
1	pound tomatoes

4	tablespoons butter
	salt and black pepper
	pinch of dried basil
4	eggs
2	tablespoons heavy cream

Trim artichoke bottoms if necessary; remove chokes and any remaining leaf nubs. If artichokes are canned, rinse them to remove canning liquid.

Peel and mince the onion. Peel and chop the tomatoes. Melt 1 tablespoon of the butter in a saucepan. Add onion and cook over low heat until soft. Add the tomatoes, salt and black pepper to taste, and the basil. Cover the pan and cook for 10 to 15 minutes. When the sauce is cooked, purée it through a food mill or in a blender. Wash out the saucepan, return the puréed sauce to it, and reheat it gently.

Break the eggs into a bowl, season with salt and pepper, and beat with a fork to blend. Sauté the artichoke hearts in 2 tablespoons butter over low heat. Melt 1 tablespoon butter in a heavy pan and pour in the eggs. Cook and stir with a wooden spoon until scrambled. Remove from heat when almost cooked, add the cream, and keep stirring until eggs are done.

Place the artichoke hearts on a warmed dish, surround with the sauce, and spoon the scrambled eggs into the artichoke bottoms.

Aijja

(Tunisian Spicy Scrambled Eggs with Sausage)

4 portions

4	medium-size green peppers
¼	teaspoon cayenne pepper
¼	teaspoon ground cuminseed
⅛	teaspoon salt
1	pound spicy sausage (hot Italian sausage or Spanish chorizos)

1	garlic clove
12	ripe plum tomatoes
2	tablespoons olive oil
¼	cup cold water
	black pepper
6	eggs

Wash peppers, quarter them, discard stems, seeds and ribs, and cut the quarters lengthwise into ½-inch-wide strips. In a small dish mix cayenne, cuminseed and salt together. Cut the sausage into 1-inch rounds. Peel and mince the garlic. Blanch and peel the tomatoes and quarter them. (If fresh plum tomatoes are not available, use 14 ounces canned peeled plum tomatoes.)

Pour the oil into a large skillet and place it over high heat. When oil is hot, add sausage slices and fry, turning often, until the sausage is browned. Pour off excess fat. Stir in the garlic, the mixture of cayenne, cuminseed and salt, the tomatoes, water and 6 grindings of black pepper. Cook over moderate heat until the mixture is thick. Stir occasionally to keep the tomatoes from sticking to the pan. Add the strips of pepper, cover the pan, and cook for another 5 minutes.

Break the eggs into a bowl and beat with a whisk to mix. Pour the eggs over the sausage mixture. Cook over low heat, stirring constantly, until the eggs are just scrambled. Do not overcook the eggs or they will become too hard and will not combine with the other ingredients. Serve *aijja* for luncheon.

Note: Tunisian dishes are spicy. You may prefer less cayenne pepper. Mint leaves are often added to this dish.

Poached Eggs Florentine

4 portions

1½ **pounds fresh spinach**	8 **poached eggs, hot**
1½ **cups béchamel sauce (see Volume 3)**	2 **ounces Parmesan cheese, grated (½ cup)**
¼ **teaspoon grated nutmeg**	

Wash and trim the spinach and blanch it in a large pot of boiling water for 5 minutes. Drain spinach, rinse with ice-cold water, and drain again. Chop the spinach in the colander and let it drain further; or purée it in a food processor fitted with the steel blade.

Pour ½ cup of the béchamel sauce into a saucepan and mix in the spinach and the nutmeg. Set the pan over moderate heat and cook, stirring constantly, for 3 to 4 min-

utes, until the sauce is hot and smooth. Preheat broiler to high.

Spoon the spinach sauce into a flameproof gratin dish. Place the poached eggs on top. Spoon remaining béchamel sauce over the eggs and sprinkle the Parmesan cheese on top. Place the gratin dish under the broiler for 3 to 4 minutes, until the top is brown and bubbly. Remove from heat and serve immediately.

Eggs Benedict

4 portions

8	thick slices of cooked ham
4	English muffins
2	tablespoons butter
8	poached eggs, hot
	Hollandaise Sauce
3	egg yolks
1	tablespoon cold water

4	ounces butter, cut into tiny pieces
¼	teaspoon salt
⅛	teaspoon cayenne pepper
1	teaspoon lemon juice
1	tablespoon light cream

Preheat broiler to high. Trim the ham slices to the same size as the muffins. Place ham on the broiler pan and broil for 2 to 3 minutes on each side. Reduce oven to 275°F. Transfer ham to an ovenproof dish and put in the oven to keep warm.

Prepare the sauce: In the top pan of a double boiler, or in a heatproof bowl set over a pan of hot water, beat the egg yolks and the water together with a wire whisk until pale and thick. Gradually beat in the butter, a few pieces at a time. Continue beating until the sauce begins to thicken. Add the salt, cayenne and lemon juice. Beat in the cream. Remove the pan from direct heat and keep the sauce warm over water no hotter than 100°F.

Split and toast the muffins and spread them with the butter. Arrange 2 muffin pieces on each of 4 warmed luncheon plates. Place a slice of ham on each muffin and top with a poached egg. Spoon a little of the sauce over each egg and serve at once for a luncheon main dish.

Poached Eggs with Broccoli

4 portions

1½	pounds fresh broccoli
2	tablespoons butter
1	teaspoon salt
½	teaspoon black pepper
1	teaspoon lemon juice

4	poached eggs, hot
½	cup dry bread crumbs
2	ounces Parmesan cheese, grated (½ cup)

Wash and trim the broccoli. Drop the stems into a saucepan of boiling water and cook for 5 minutes. Add the flower heads and cook for 5 to 8 minutes longer, until both stems and florets are very tender. Drain, rinse with cold water, and drain again. Put the broccoli through a food mill or purée in a blender or in a food processor fitted with the steel blade. (The food mill will retain any fibers, giving a smoother purée.) Turn the purée into a saucepan and warm it over low heat, stirring constantly.

Preheat broiler to high. Spread the broccoli purée in a heatproof serving dish. Dot with 1 tablespoon of the butter and sprinkle with salt, pepper and lemon juice. Arrange poached eggs on the broccoli and cover eggs with bread crumbs and grated cheese. Dot with remaining tablespoon of butter. Place the dish under the broiler for 5 minutes, until the top is golden brown. Remove dish from the broiler and serve immediately.

Poached Eggs in Aspic "Jeannette"

4 portions

4 eggs
1½ cups jellied chicken consommé
2 tablespoons Madeira or sherry

4 tablespoons butter
2 tablespoons heavy cream
8 ounces pâté de foie gras or other good-quality liver pâté

Poach the eggs and keep them in cold water. Turn the consommé into a saucepan and melt it over gentle heat. Stir in the Madeira or sherry and let the consommé become cold. Put the butter in a bowl and cream it with a wooden spoon until it is completely smooth, but not melted. Add the cream and pâté and mix thoroughly. Put the pâté mixture into a piping bag fitted with a medium-size star nozzle and pipe out a thin base of the pâté in the bottom of 4 ramekins or individual soufflé dishes.

Lift the eggs out of the cold water and carefully blot them dry. Place 1 egg in each ramekin on the pâté base. Pipe a circle of the pâté around the eggs so they stay firmly in place, centered in the ramekins. Carefully fill each ramekin with the cooled consommé. Place the dishes in the refrigerator for several hours to set. Serve as a first course.

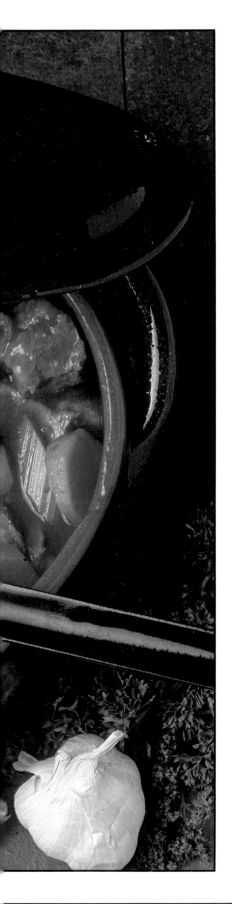

Part Two

MOIST-HEAT COOKING MEATS

Braising and pot-roasting are the two main moist methods for cooking meats. In essence, they are the opposite of broiling and roasting. When meats are braised or pot-roasted, they are cooked in tightly covered pots, very slowly, over a relatively long period of time. This long slow process tenderizes the meat and makes this cooking method an ideal way to deal with the less tender (and usually less expensive) cuts of meat.

In both methods, the meat is initially browned or seared. For braising, the meat is placed on a bed of flavoring vegetables called a *mirepoix,* and some liquid is added. The liquid may be strained marinade, stock or simply water. Pot-roasting follows the procedure with the elimination of the *mirepoix,* and only a very small amount of liquid is called for. Vegetables can be added to the pot-roasting meat, but these are usually timed so that the meat and vegetables are tender and ready to be served together.

The secret of success in both methods rests on using the right pot. It must be a heavy pot with a tight-fitting cover; the size is important because the meat should fit snugly inside. Too much space in the pot will cause the liquid to become steam, thus diluting the mixture, and evaporating. The aim is to concentrate the heat around the meat in such a way that juices inside are slowly extracted. In effect, the meat cooks in its own juices and becomes tender and well flavored. The small amount of liquid in the pot becomes a thickly gelatinous and richly flavored sauce.

The word "braise" comes from the French *braiser,* which means to cook in smoldering coals in a special pot called a *braisière* (also *daubière*). This is a heavy metal pot with a deeply indented and very tight-fitting lid. The pot was set upon a bed of embers and more glowing embers were heaped onto the concave lid. Today we can achieve the same effect by braising in the oven, but the correct cooking utensil is still extremely important.

The same cuts of meat that produce such excellent results when they are pot-roasted or braised can be cut up into smaller pieces to become a stew. Stews and casseroles are prepared in the same fashion as braised meats, although, generally, stews use more liquid.

Stews, ragouts, daubes, pot roasts and casseroles are well-established dishes that appear in myriad versions all over the world. They form the cornerstone of a particular type of family cooking. As Richard Olney poetically expresses it, "they embody—or spark—something akin to an ancestral or racial memory of farmhouse kitchens—of rustic tables laid by mothers, grandmothers, or old retainers" *(Simple French Food)*.

Not surprisingly, many of the world's most celebrated stewed or moist-baked dishes are named for the pots they are cooked in—*cassoulet, daube, tagine, tian,* and of course casserole. This last word, which simply means any sort of round saucepan or baking dish in French, has been adopted into American usage to denote any cooking-and-serving vessel used to hold a baked main dish.

The word "stew" itself seems to have wandered into modern usage by odd paths. It is thought to derive from a Late Latin or Middle French word for a heated bath or public bathhouse; the latter tended to be of dubious enough reputation to have given rise to the Middle English word "stews." Stewing is indeed a kind of combination of a water bath and a steam bath, a prolonged version of both poaching and stewing that breaks down some components of food over a period of hours to produce a tender consistency and help promote exchange of flavors.

Trying to discern some logical order in the names of the classic stewed or moist-baked dishes is a hopeless cause. Roughly speaking, stews and allied preparations fall into two categories: those in which the ingredients are cooked *à blanc*—placed directly in the cooking liquid—and those in which all or some are cooked *à brun*—sautéed or browned first. (Stewing *à brun* is often known as braising.) Some authorities strictly reserve some names, for example *fricassée,* for the first category only; others apply them to both types.

Other distinctions that could be the basis of strict categories but have never been systematically applied are those between rich stews with a small amount of liquid and thin ones with a lot of soupy liquid, or those bound with some thickening agent and those that contain only the natural cooking juices.

A mere sampling of French stews will give some idea of the overall size and variety of preparations that fall into this category.

Ragoût is the general French name for a stew, but many celebrated braised or long-simmered dishes tend to be known individually by descriptive names, such as *coq au vin, tripes à la mode de Caen,* or *boeuf bourguignon,* so that the word *ragoût* does not appear in cookbooks or menu listings as often as one might expect. *Fricassée* is often used as a general name for stews of poultry cooked *à blanc,* but a look through a few cookbooks will quickly reveal many fricassees in which all or some of the ingredients are first sautéed in butter or oil, as well as many that use veal, lamb, rabbit, and other meats.

The word that gave rise to the English "stew"—*estouffade*—is still in use, but it is now a somewhat amorphous term referring either to slowly cooked stews or pot roasts of various sorts, or to the stock in which they cook. *Blanquettes* are a particular family of stews usually made from delicate, tender meats like veal or chicken first cooked in stock, then combined with cooked small onions and mushrooms, and finally thickened with a liaison of cream and egg yolks. Some fricassees also receive final enrichment. A *civet* is usually made of small game, simmered in a red-wine sauce thickened with the animal's blood; a *navarin* is a mutton or lamb stew, sometimes cooked with an assortment of spring vegetables *(à la printanière)*. But both of these last terms are also confusingly applied to seafood preparations.

Cassoulet, the celebrated Languedoc bean casserole, is indeed a formidable affair. Though it is basically a simple dish, the sheer number of meats involved in full-scale versions means complex logistics. Various towns claim it as their own, vociferously disagreeing with the approach of neighbors. At its most minimal, *cassoulet* is much like an unsweetened version of our own baked-bean dishes: white beans gently cooked at very low heat for many hours, with bacon or salt pork, in an earthenware *cassole*—the Languedoc equivalent of the beanpot, which has given its name to the dish. More often it contains a few pieces of fresh goose or browned lamb and/or pork. Sometimes garlic sausage is added with or without fresh pork-sausage cakes. A layer of bread crumbs is sprinkled over the whole, forming a rich crust as the dish bakes. Assembling these ingredients, browning the stewing meats, and preparing the stock in which everything is to cook is a task, but there is no doubt that the results are worth it.

Though other nations have sometimes adopted some of the French names for stewed dishes, virtually every part of Europe clings to its own ideas on the making of stews. Some travel well; others are hard to recreate outside their own region. Irish stew and its close relative, Lancashire hotpot, are mutton or lamb stews of a somewhat austere stripe. They are cooked *à blanc* and at their most threadbare have been known to contain nothing except sliced potatoes, an onion or two, a few pieces of lamb or mutton, and as much water as possible. On this side of the Atlantic, traditional recipes for these venerable dishes rarely produce memorable results. But when made with truly flavorful potatoes and good mutton chops they abundantly justify their simplicity.

Hungarian *gulyás* or goulash is another traveler that is rarely appreciated on its original terms. True *gulyás* is a very simple stew, innocent of expensive mystery ingredients and complex seasonings. Like Irish stew, it is usually moistened with water instead of stock, a practice that new converts to *haute cuisine* often assume is quite beneath them. It does, however, demand good flavorful stewing meat (usually beef, though any other stewing meat or combination of meats can be used) and real Hungarian paprika, and precisely because it is so simple, it will have little real savor if made with inferior ingredients.

A somewhat different problem of authenticity is presented by the famous Jewish dish *cholent* (also spelled *tscholent* or *schalet*). It is something like a very simple *cassoulet:* well-seasoned beans slowly baked with stewing beef or goose. Formerly it was the standard Saturday dinner of Eastern European Jews who could not light their own cooking fires on the Sabbath; the dish was therefore made up on Friday and taken to the village bread oven, where it was left to bake overnight in the banked fires and collected the next day.

In America, stews and related dishes have long had an association with no-nonsense, stick-to-the-ribs cooking because they lend themselves to one-pot meals that can be done over a campfire or made up in vast quantities and served to multitudes. Kentucky burgoo, a hunters' stew in which whatever anyone has bagged (wild duck, squirrel, rabbit, or other catch) is thrown into the kettle along with various fresh vegetables (and maybe a chicken or some stewing beef) is about the most heroic example, but not the only one. On a more modest scale there is Brunswick stew, a kindred Southern specialty based on squirrel (chicken is often substituted today) and an assortment of vegetables. The potpies of the Pennsylvania Dutch (which can be made of chicken, veal, or beef) are nothing but thick stews with the addition of home-made noodle dough cut into squares; Louisiana gumbos are a kind of stew, as are many versions of that favorite southwest dish, *chile con carne.*

Braised meats, succulent pot roasts, stews, casseroles—all can be hearty, simple fare or elegant dishes suitable for any occasion. The one ingredient that they all must have in common in order to succeed is slow, gentle, unhurried cooking in a well-covered pot that's not too big.

BRAISING, POT-ROASTING, STEWING

When properly cooked, the less tender cuts of meat often have more flavor along with a melt-in-the-mouth succulence and tenderness.

Choosing the Meat

The following cuts of meat are good choices for braising, pot-roasting and stewing:

Beef

Chuck Arm Pot Roast. This cut contains a round arm bone and sometimes cross sections of rib bones. There are several different muscles and connective tissue. A piece 3 to 5 pounds will need 2½ to 3½ hours of cooking to be tender. Other cuts of the chuck, with bones or boneless, will require the same time.

Chuck Cross-Rib Pot Roast. This cut contains rib bones, but it may be boned, rolled and tied. Layers of fat in this cut keep the meat moist. In a good grade the meat will be tender. Allow 2½ to 3 hours for a 3- to 5-pound cut.

Chuck Blade Roast. This cut contains blade bone, backbone, rib bone and various muscles. It is usually cut 2 inches thick. A piece weighing 3 pounds will require 2½ to 3 hours.

Shank Crosscuts. These are also called shin of beef. This cut is very nutritious, rich in gelatin, and the bone contains a disc of marrow. Shank does best with a cold start. Allow about 3 hours for these to become tender (a good cut for the slow cooker). When

meat is tender, pull off and discard the membranes between the sections of meat; be sure to add the marrow to the stew.

Brisket. This cut is boneless, but it contains layers of fat. You will need to skim the liquid well; or prepare a day ahead so that the fat rises and can be lifted off. A piece of 4 to 5 pounds will require 3½ to 4½ hours from a cold start, but will provide at least 10 portions.

Round Rump Roast. A large piece containing the aitchbone and three round muscles. If the meat is of good grade, this will be delicious braised or pot-roasted. A piece of about 5 pounds will require about 2½ hours. Brown the meat first.

Round Bottom Round Roast. This is the perfect cut to braise or pot-roast whole. The shape is somewhat irregular, so the initial browning needs care. Other cuts from the round (the eye, tip and rump round) are also good. A piece of 5 pounds will require about 3 hours.

Veal

Shoulder Arm Roast. This piece contains a good many bones and various muscles. A piece of 3 to 4 pounds will require about 3 hours. It will not be easy to carve, and it requires care to prevent drying.

Veal Cubes. These tender pieces are cut from the shoulder, breast, flank and shanks and make excellent stews; 1-to-2 inch cubes need only 1½ hours to be fully cooked. Cuts taken from the flank and shanks release gelatin, providing added richness.

Leg Rump Roast. Like a beef rump roast. Brown it well and be sure to use a good vegetable mixture to give flavor and moisture. A piece of 4 to 5 pounds will require about 2½ hours.

Lamb

Shank. A flavorful delicious piece. If these weigh more than ¾ pound, ask your butcher to crack the

Beef Chuck Arm Pot Roast

Beef Brisket

Veal Cubes

bone. Shanks require about 1½ hours, and can be cooked longer to release more gelatin. Each one will make 2 portions. Braise, pot-roast or stew. A good choice for the slow cooker.

Lamb Cubes. For stews, these are cut mostly from the neck, shank and breast. Cubes of 1½ inches should be cooked for 1 to 1½ hours. For a

29

Beef Cuts, Veal Cuts, Lamb Cuts

Beef Chuck Cross-Rib Pot Roast

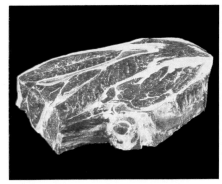

Beef Chuck Blade Roast

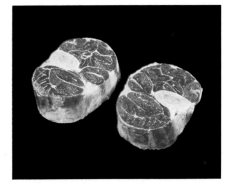

Beef Shank Crosscuts

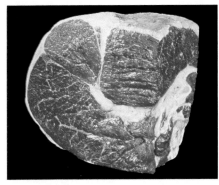

Beef Round Rump Roast

Beef Round Bottom Round Roast

Veal Shoulder Arm Roast

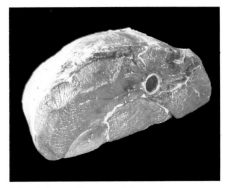

Veal Leg Rump Roast

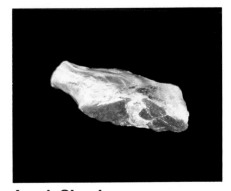

Lamb Shank

Lamb Cubes

special occasion a leg may be boned and cubed; this meat is more tender and can also be skewered and broiled.

Pork

Shoulder Arm Steak. Cut like a thick steak. A piece 1½ to 2 inches thick will need 1½ to 2 hours, but be sure to test as pork should not be over-cooked. Add a little oil to the *mirepoix* for braising.

Country-Style Ribs. These are made by splitting the blade end of the loin. Although they contain bones, they also contain a thick layer of meat. A piece of 1½ pounds will be deliciously tender in 1½ hours. Braise rather than pot-roast.

Pork Cubes. Since pork is slaughtered young, it is generally tender, and cubes already cut for sale can be a good choice for stew or casserole. They may be cut from any meaty section. Cubes of 1½ inches will be tender in 1 hour. They can also be braised.

Pork Shoulder Arm Steak

Pork Country-Style Ribs

Pork Cubes

A Glossary of Terms

Braising, pot-roasting and stewing cover such enormous culinary ground that it may be useful to have the following glossary on hand.

Blanquette. A French white stew, made of chicken, veal or rabbit, simmered in unthickened stock or other liquid. When the meat is tender, the liquid is thickened with a liaison of egg yolks and cream. Mushrooms are often added.

Carbonnade. A Flemish stew of beef or pork, made with ale or beer as part of the liquid and always including browned or sautéed onions.

Casserole. In France, simply a saucepan. An earthenware saucepan is a *casserole en terre,* but special saucepans or pots for specific uses have their own names. The dish we call a casserole, in France a *cocotte,* is a deep round or oval cooking pot with a tight-fitting lid with small handles on each side. This may be earthenware or cast iron or ceramic-coated iron or steel, etc. A casserole can be used on top of the stove or in the oven. In our usage, the food cooked in one of these pots is also called a casserole (chicken casserole, etc.).

Daube. A Provençal stew baked in a sturdy pot that is sealed with a flour and water paste. After the cooking starts, the pot is never opened until the end. The meat is cut into chunks or strips, but it is not browned first. It rests between thick layers of vegetables. Beef is the most used meat, but tripe is also cooked in a *daube.*

Eintopf. A German casserole made of meat or fish and vegetables. Everything is cut into small pieces and the ingredients are layered in the casserole. The meat can be browned or not.

Estouffade. Similar to a *daube;* the pot is sealed. The meat cooks in its own liquid; one might call it "smothering." The term *étuvée* means almost the same thing, although some liquid may be added for cooking *à l'étuvée.*

Fonds de Braise. The mixture of *mirepoix* vegetables with a *bouquet garni* and a large piece of blanched pork rind or a calf's foot or pig's foot, split, used to add gelatin and flavor to the meat.

Fricassée. A white stew; it differs from a *blanquette* in that the meat is first seared, usually in butter, but not browned, and it may also be floured so that thickening at the end is not necessary. The liquid may be water or stock.

Goulash. A Hungarian stew made of meat and onions cooked in lard or bacon fat until most of the liquid has evaporated. Vegetables are sometimes added toward the end, especially peppers and potatoes. Paprika, hot or sweet, is always used, but sour cream is never added to a true Hungarian *gulyás.* The meat may be beef, mutton, veal or pork.

Mirepoix. A mixture of flavoring vegetables, usually carrots and onions, but leeks, celery and parsley may be added. All the pieces are cut into even cubes, 1/6 to 1/4 inch thick. The *mirepoix* is often browned in butter. It is used as a bed (part of the *fonds de braise*) on which the meat or poultry rests for braising or stewing.

Navarin. A French stew of lamb or mutton. The meat is browned first, as in braising. Tiny spring vegetables should be used—carrots, turnips, onions and potatoes. At other seasons, cut larger specimens into balls.

Paprikás. A "dry-stewed" Hungarian dish of veal, chicken or fish, including onions and paprika. Heavy sweet cream or sour cream is added toward the end of the cooking.

Ragoût. A French stew. The ingredients should be cooked for a long time and the final result must be savory. The chief ingredient may be meat, poultry or game.

Equipment

For braising and pot-roasting you will need a heavy pan that is just large enough to hold the meat. It must have a tight-fitting cover.

If your pot is much larger than the meat, compensate by covering the meat with a thick sheet of aluminum foil, folded so as to form a shallow basin over the food. As steam rises and condenses on the lid of the pot, it will fall into the foil basin, without diluting the juices of the braise. The foil container is emptied before you serve the food.

Another problem may arise if you have a pot of the right size and shape that is not flameproof. In that case, sear the meat and sauté the *mirepoix* in a heavy skillet and transfer them to the pot to braise in the oven or over an asbestos pad at low temperature on top of the stove.

Marinades

An excellent way of tenderizing and adding flavor to meat, particularly to the coarser cuts, is to marinate the meat for 1 to 2 days before cooking.

If you choose to marinate the meat to give it more flavor, prepare about 1 cup marinade for each pound of meat. For the acid use wine, or vinegar and water, or citrus juices. Add oil, herbs, spices, flavoring vegetables. Mix all together and pour over the meat in a glass or ceramic container. For flavoring, soak for 2 hours. For tenderizing, soak for up to 2 days, turning the meat often. However, if you continue the process for more than a few hours, the meat will taste "sour" like the classic *sauerbraten;* the natural meat taste will be obscured.

Braising

Choose your meat and choose a pot of the right size for it. If your meat is very lean, you may wish to lard it. If your meat is very fatty, trim it as thoroughly as possible; internal layers of fat will remain and these will be "melted" during cooking.

You may choose to marinate the meat but it is not essential for meats to be braised. Prepare the *fonds de braise.* Blanch a piece of pork rind or a pig's foot (if the taste of pork is agreeable to the dish); or split and blanch a

calf's foot. Use pig's foot or calf's foot only if the braising will take a long time, as gelatin in these joints is extracted only after long cooking. Trim, wash, and dice vegetables into a *mirepoix.* Sauté them in a little vegetable oil or some of the fat cut from the meat or in butter.

Brown the meat. If it has been marinated, pat it completely dry first. Browning may be done in the braising pot if it is flameproof, but it is easier to do it in a heavy skillet, as turning in the skillet is easier; also there is no possibility of steaming in the more open pan. Use enough fat in either pot to cover the bottom and prevent sticking. Turn the meat with wooden spoons to brown evenly on all sides. Discard all the fat.

An alternative method, which is good for meats with a lot of internal fats: Put the meat in a covered oven dish and bake in a 350°F oven for 1 to 1½ hours. The oven browning can be done a day ahead. When the meat is browned, much of the internal and external fat will be released. Discard all the fat. With either method of browning, deglaze the pan with stock or wine and add the liquid to the braising pot.

Arrange pork rind and *mirepoix* in the braising pot. Add *bouquet garni* or other herbs. Place browned meat on top. Pour in the deglazing. Add also the strained marinade if you used it, or part of it. Or pour in about ½ cup stock, wine or water. Cover pot tightly. Set it over low heat on top of the stove, or put in a 325°F oven, and cook for about 20 minutes per pound. Open the pot and turn the meat over. If the liquid has cooked away, add another ½ cup, very hot. Cover and continue to cook until the meat is very tender; if there are bones, meat should be separating from them. Lift meat to a warmed plate and keep warm. Skim fat from the juices in the pan. For a simple quick sauce, discard *bouquet garni* or bay leaf and pork rind, and purée the juices and vegetables in a food processor fitted with the steel blade, or force the mixture through a food mill or sieve. You may need to thin the purée with a little stock. Season it. If the mixture is

too thin for a sauce, thicken it with a cornstarch slurry or gently stir in some *beurre manié* (tiny amounts of butter and flour kneaded together).

Pot-Roasting

Prepare the meat in the same fashion as for braising. If it has been marinated, pat it completely dry before browning. Tie the meat if necessary. Brown meat on all sides in fat or oil. Pour off the fat. Season the meat, and add any herbs or spices. Pour in 1 or 2 cups liquid. Bring the liquid to a boil on top of the stove, then cover closely and cook, still on top of the stove, or in a preheated 325°F oven, for the time the meat needs. About 1 hour before the meat is done, add whole onions, carrots, parsnips, small turnips, and continue cooking until meat and vegetables are done. Look at the pot roast at least once an hour and add more hot liquid, ½ cup at a time, if needed.

Stewing

Good stews are made in the same fashion as good braises and pot roasts. The differences are that the meats used are cut into pieces, more liquid is used, and not all meats begin with browning.

You may use a cold start for any stew if you prefer. As the name cold-start implies, this method of stewing or casseroling involves long slow cooking starting from cold, and it cannot be hurried.

It is the only method which successfully tenderizes the coarsest, muscular cuts of meat. If you attempted to cook these cuts by the fry-start method, the rapid heat involved in browning the meat would cause the sinews to contract and harden so much that no amount of subsequent gentle simmering would produce really tender results.

In this method cold liquid is added to cold meat and other stew ingredients, and the whole is very slowly brought to a simmer and allowed to continue for as long as it takes to be-

Braising Meat

3 pounds meat
3 tablespoons fat or oil

Marinade

1 onion
1 carrot
1 garlic clove
1 cup wine
1 bouquet garni
6 peppercorns

Mirepoix

4 onions
6 carrots
6 to 8 celery ribs

Gravy

1 cup stock
2 tablespoons cornstarch

1 Chop onion and carrot for marinade; crush garlic. Combine with wine, bouquet garni and peppercorns in a glass container.

2 Lard meat, or remove excess fat. Put meat in the marinade and let it rest in a cool place for several hours, turning often.

6 Place meat on the vegetable bed. Pour in strained marinade and add stock to reach two thirds of the depth of the mirepoix.

7 Cover pot tightly. Braise in the center of the oven. Check during cooking that the liquid is just simmering.

8 When meat is tender, remove it from the casserole and keep it warm. Skim fat from the juices in the casserole.

come tender. Do not let the liquid evaporate; ideally you should not need to add more.

Cold-start stews and casseroles are usually unthickened—except where potatoes disintegrate during cooking and naturally thicken the liquid. The omission of flour means that the liquid can penetrate meat fibers more easily, reducing tough sinews to

a jellylike texture and tenderizing the meat muscle. During this process the flavorsome juices are drawn from the meat into the small amount of added liquid, to produce a rich meaty gravy.

Casseroles

A casserole is a dish like a stew, usually baked in the oven, but it has relatively

little liquid when it is done; everything is deliciously moist but not soupy. An important consideration for casserole cooking is that everything in the casserole is part of the finished dish. Therefore, if the meat is to be browned, be sure to do it in a skillet so that all excess fat can be eliminated.

Use a 325°F oven for most casseroles. If the contents seem pale, un-

3 Preheat oven to 325°F. Remove meat from marinade and pat it completely dry with paper towels.

4 Heat the fat in a flameproof casserole or in a skillet. Brown meat on all sides over high heat. Remove from pan and keep warm.

5 Peel and dice onions and carrots for mirepoix. Wash and dice celery. Brown vegetables gently in fat remaining in the casserole.

9 For a thin gravy, add some stock to the casserole. Season mixture well. Strain juices to remove vegetables.

10 For thicker gravy, mix cornstarch with cold water. Warm with a little of the pan juices, add to casserole and cook until thickened.

11 Cut meat into thick slices and arrange on a platter with vegetables. Spoon some gravy over, and serve the rest separately.

cover the pot toward the end, increase oven heat to 375° to 400°F, and let the meat brown, turning it and basting with butter and pan juices as needed.

Reheating Casseroles and Stews

Unlike roasted or fried meat dishes, casseroles and stews reheat extremely well. If anything, flavors tend to intensify and mellow, so it makes good sense to cook at least enough for two meals at one time, and if you have a freezer, a good deal more. Always cool the casserole as quickly as possible before refrigerating or freezing. This means moving the quantity to be frozen straight into the foil-lined container(s) or freezer box(es) of appropri-

ate size. It will cool quicker in a smaller container. When cold, cover and put in the freezer. Always leave ½″ head space to allow for expansion.

Reheating should be done slowly. Taking the casserole straight from the refrigerator and subjecting it to fierce heat will toughen the meat, however tender the original cooked results. Whenever possible, bring the casse-

6 portions

2 pounds beef chuck or blade
4 tablespoons flour
  salt and pepper
2 onions
2 carrots
1 parsnip, turnip or small
    rutabaga
3 tablespoons beef drippings
    or vegetable oil
2 cups light beef stock or water
1 tablespoon tomato purée
1 bouquet garni (thyme,
    parsley, bay leaf)

1 Trim fat and skin from meat. Cut meat into 1½-inch cubes. Preheat oven to 325°F.

2 Mix flour with seasoning to taste. Put flour in a plastic bag and shake the meat, a few pieces at a time, to coat well.

5 Heat fat in a flameproof casserole. Brown the floured meat cubes, a few at a time, until all are browned all over.

6 Transfer each batch of meat to a plate. Use a slotted spoon, so that the fat remains in the pan.

7 Reduce heat slightly. Add onion slices and sauté until golden brown, stirring to brown evenly.

10 Return pan to the heat, bring the liquid mixture to a boil, and cook, stirring, until smooth.

11 Remove pan from heat and add meat and bouquet garni. Cover tightly and simmer in the center of the oven for 1 hour.

12 Add root vegetables to the stew, pushing them into the sauce. Simmer for another 1 to 1½ hours.

3 Set floured cubes on a plate and continue to shake the cubes until all are coated. Reserve remaining flour.

4 Peel vegetables and cut them into slices or cubes.

8 Stir in remaining seasoned flour. Cook over low heat, stirring all the time, until the roux is nut brown.

9 Heat stock or water and stir in tomato purée. Pour mixture slowly into the roux, off the heat, and mix until well combined.

13 Remove any fat from the surface of the liquid with a skimmer or paper towels.

14 Check the meat to be sure it is done. Adjust seasoning if necessary. Serve from the casserole.

role to room temperature before beginning the reheating process. Always reheat over gentle heat or in a medium-low oven, bringing the casserole slowly back to simmering point. Then maintain a gentle simmer for 10 minutes or so before serving.

Cooking with Beer, Wine and Spirits

Braises, pot roasts, stews and casseroles often include some alcoholic beverage as part of the liquid. Beer of various kinds, ale and stout are all used in stews. Table wines, the kind you drink with meals, are fine for cooking. The better the wine, the better the dish. Red wines are natural with beef and lamb, but occasionally red is used with chicken and veal. White is the wine of choice with pork, also with fish and most poultry dishes. Rosé is less flavorful than red and white, but you may use it almost like beer. Any of these wines are added to the dish with the other liquid, so there is ample time for the alcohol to evaporate and the flavor to become concentrated.

Fortified wines—sherry, port, Madeira, Marsala—have already been "reduced" in the process of manufacture. Apéritif wines—vermouth, Dubonnet, etc.—are wines that have been flavored with herbs or herbal extracts, so they must be used cautiously.

Using liqueurs is rather different. The alcoholic content is much higher and the flavor intense. A few tablespoons may give a special touch. More often these are used for flaming the meat of the stew.

The liqueur for flaming must be heated. Do this in a separate pan or a ladle. Pour it over the food and ignite it, or ignite and pour it flaming over the food. For safety, always ignite with a taper so you are not on top of the alcohol as it flares up. Also, never pour alcohol from the bottle into a hot mixture. Rather, pour the needed amount into a cup, pitcher or ladle, away from the heat, and then heat just the amount you need.

Cold-Start Braising or Stewing

1 Wipe the meat. Cut away excess fat and tough outside skin. If baking the stew, preheat the oven to 325°F.

2 Cut meat across the grain into 1½-inch cubes.

3 Peel and trim onions, carrots, turnips, and other hard vegetables. Cut into even slices or cubes, or leave whole.

4 Place meat in the stewpot or casserole. Add vegetables, herbs and cold liquid, 1 cup liquid for each pound of meat.

5 Season meat. Cover pot tightly and bring slowly to a simmer, either on top of the stove or in the oven.

6 Maintain a gentle simmer throughout. If the liquid seems to be boiling, whether on the stove or in the oven, reduce heat.

7 Check at intervals to be sure liquid remains at a simmer, or to add more liquid if needed.

8 When meat is tender, remove it to a warm plate. Skim off surface fat with paper towel.

OR If you have time, let the stew become cold, then lift off the solidified fat on the top. Reheat to serve.

Boeuf à la Mode (Braised Beef in Aspic)

6 portions

1	rump of beef, 3 to 4½ pounds
4	ounces salt pork, cut into ¼-inch strips
3	onions
4	large carrots
3	pig's feet
3	tablespoons oil
½	cup brandy
	salt and black pepper
2½	cups brown stock
24	baby carrots
	parsley sprigs

Marinade

1	onion
1	carrot
1	garlic clove
1½	cups red wine
4	parsley sprigs
1	bay leaf
1	teaspoon dried thyme
12	peppercorns

This traditional *bourgeois* French dish can be served hot or cold.
• To serve cold, begin marinating the meat 2 days in advance.

• To serve hot, begin a day before serving; simply surround the sliced meat with the carrots, spooning the degreased broth over.
• This is one case where canned broth cannot be substituted for stock; the pig's feet lend gelatinous body for the aspic. Have your butcher split them for you.
• Test firmness of aspic by putting a spoonful onto a chilled saucer; freeze for 5 minutes. If broth is not firm enough to gel when cold, reduce it over high heat by a quarter of its volume; test again.

Boeuf à la Mode (Braised Beef in Aspic) (continued)

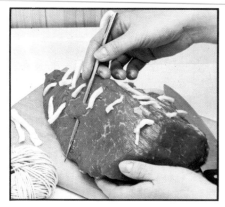

1 Lard meat with strips of salt pork and tie into a neat, compact shape, if necessary.

2 For marinade, peel and chop onion and carrot; peel and crush garlic. Add wine, herbs and peppercorns.

3 Place meat in a bowl with marinade. Leave in a cool place or refrigerator to marinate overnight, turning occasionally.

7 Warm brandy in small saucepan. Ladle over meat, carefully setting light to the last ladleful as you pour it.

8 Lift meat partially. Scatter carrots and pig's feet under and around meat. Season with salt and black pepper to taste.

9 Strain marinade into pan. Add stock to cover meat. If not enough, add water or more stock.

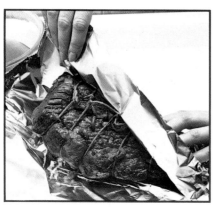

13 Wrap meat in foil and chill. Put bowl of liquid in refrigerator for at least 4 hours or overnight.

14 Scrape baby carrots and boil them in salted water until tender. Drain and leave to cool.

15 Remove layer of fat from the liquid. Check that the aspic is of firm consistency.

4 Remove meat from marinade and blot dry. Preheat oven to 300°F. Place rack in lower third of oven.

5 Peel and dice onions and large carrots. Scrub pig's feet clean in cold water and cut into pieces.

6 Heat oil in flameproof casserole in which meat fits snugly. Brown onions, add meat and brown all sides over high heat.

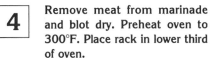

10 Bring to boil. Put lid on casserole and cook in center of oven for 4 to 5 hours.

11 Check after 30 minutes that meat is simmering. If necessary, reduce heat. Meat should not boil.

12 Remove meat to separate dish to cool, loosely covered with foil. Strain pan juices through cheesecloth into a bowl. Cool.

16 Cut aspic into pieces and warm to liquefy. Leave until syrupy and beginning to set.

17 Meanwhile, cut meat into thick slices. Arrange overlapping on serving platter. Garnish with cold baby carrots and parsley.

18 Pour the thick liquid over the meat and carrots and leave in the refrigerator until cold.

Carbonnade à la Flamande

(Flemish Beef Stew with Beer)

6 portions

2	pounds beef chuck or round
1	pound onions
3	garlic cloves
3	tablespoons vegetable oil
1	teaspoon salt
¼	teaspoon black pepper

½	cup strong beef stock
1½	cups slightly sour beer or ale
1	tablespoon brown sugar
1	bouquet garni
1	tablespoon cornstarch
1½	tablespoons wine vinegar

Trim meat and discard excess fat. Pat dry with paper towels. Cut meat into strips 2 × 3 inches. Peel onions and cut into thin slices. Peel garlic and put through a press.

Heat the oil in a large skillet; add half of the meat strips and brown quickly on all sides over high heat. Remove with a slotted spoon to a large saucepan. Brown remaining meat and transfer to the saucepan. Reduce heat to moderate and stir the onions into the oil remaining in the skillet. Cook for 6 to 8 minutes, stirring frequently, until slightly browned. Stir in garlic, salt and pepper, and cook for 1 minute. Spoon the onion mixture into the saucepan of beef. Pour stock and beer or ale into the skillet and stir in the sugar. Stir until the skillet is deglazed, then pour the deglazing into the saucepan. Bury the *bouquet garni* in the meat strips. Bring the liquid to a gentle boil. Cover the pan tightly and simmer for 2½ hours, until the meat is very tender.

Skim off any surface fat. Blend cornstarch and vinegar in a cup and stir the slurry into the saucepan, stirring all the time. Simmer, still stirring, until the sauce is thickened, a few minutes only. Adjust the seasonings and serve.

Daube de Boeuf à la Provençale

(Beef Stew with Olives)

6 to 8 portions

3	pounds beef rump
8	ounces smoked bacon, about 10 strips
8	ounces mushrooms
1½	pounds tomatoes
3	garlic cloves
20	oil-cured black olives
1	cup flour
1	strip of dried orange rind, about 6 inches long
1	bouquet garni
¾	cup beef stock

Marinade

4	medium-size onions
4	medium-size carrots
1¼	cups dry white wine
¼	cup brandy
2	garlic cloves
2	teaspoons coarse salt
6	black peppercorns
1	bay leaf
½	teaspoon crumbled dried thyme

Have the beef cut into 2-inch cubes. Make the marinade: Peel onions and scrape carrots and cut both into thin slices. Put vegetables in a large bowl and pour in the wine and brandy. Peel garlic cloves and crush them with the coarse salt. Crack the peppercorns in a mortar. Add these ingredients, the bay leaf and the thyme to the marinade and stir well. Add the beef cubes and turn them to moisten thoroughly. Cover the bowl and marinate the beef in the refrigerator for at least 12 hours, turning the meat occasionally.

Cut the bacon strips into 1-inch pieces and simmer them in a large pot of water for 10 minutes. Drain them and pat dry with paper towels. Wipe mushrooms with a damp cloth, trim the base of the stems, and slice caps and stems. Blanch and peel the tomatoes, press out as many seeds as possible, and chop the tomatoes. Peel garlic cloves and put through a press into the tomatoes. Pit the olives and cut them into halves. Assemble the *bouquet garni*: use 4 parsley sprigs, 1 thyme sprig and 1 bay leaf; tie herbs together.

Remove beef cubes from the marinade and dry them on paper towels. Strain the marinade into a bowl, reserving both the liquid and the vegetables. Discard the bay leaf. Preheat oven to 325°F. Put the flour in a bowl and dip the beef cubes into it until they are well coated; shake the pieces in a strainer to remove excess flour. Scatter some of the blanched bacon strips on the bottom of a *daubière* or a large flameproof casserole. Next spoon in a layer of the marinated vegetables, the chopped tomatoes and sliced mushrooms. Add a layer of the beef pieces. Put the orange rind and the *bouquet garni* in next. Continue making layers of bacon, vegetables and beef, ending with bacon. Pour in the beef stock, the strained marinade, and scatter the olives on top.

Seal the lid of the pot in place with a paste of flour and water so no moisture can escape from the pot. Set the casserole in the center of the oven and braise the stew for about 4 hours, without opening the pot. After that time, test the meat; it should be very tender.

Remove the pot from the oven, open it, and skim any fat from the top surface. Discard the *bouquet garni* and the strip of orange rind. The daube will remain hot for some time, so it can be served at your convenience, and it is therefore an excellent dish for a buffet meal.

Variations: The olives, garlic and tomatoes are typical of Provençal cooking; for a plain beef daube, omit them. For a daube in the style of Avignon, use lamb and omit mushrooms and tomatoes; add rosemary and allspice to the marinade. In Béarn, the daube includes ham and often goose.

42

Gulyás
(Hungarian Beef Goulash)

6 portions

2 pounds boneless beef from
  chuck or round
1 pound onions
2 tablespoons lard
1 garlic clove
1 teaspoon caraway seeds

salt
2 tablespoons paprika
2 cups water, very warm
2 large tomatoes
2 green peppers

Have the beef cut into 1-inch cubes. Peel and chop onions. Melt the lard in a heavy flameproof casserole. Cook the chopped onions in the lard over low heat until soft and translucent. Add the beef cubes and cook for about 15 minutes, until beef has lost its red color. Stir all the while to mix beef and onions. Peel garlic and put through a press into the beef. Crush caraway seeds in a mortar and add to the casserole with 1 teaspoon salt and the paprika. Stir with a wooden spoon to mix well, then pour in the warm water. Cover the casserole and simmer over low heat for 1 hour.

Blanch and peel the tomatoes and chop them. Char the peppers and remove skins, or peel them with a vegetable peeler. Discard stems, seeds and ribs, and chop peppers.

Uncover goulash and stir in the chopped tomatoes and peppers. If all the water has evaporated, add a little more, ½ cup at a time, being sure it is very warm. Add another ½ teaspoon salt. Cover and simmer for 30 to 40 minutes longer. The stew should be moist but not soupy. Serve with noodles, spaetzle or dumplings.

Boeuf à la Bourguignonne
(Beef Stew in Red Wine)

6 portions

8 strips of smoked bacon
3 pounds boneless beef for
  stew
1 carrot
1 onion
3 garlic cloves
1 tablespoon olive oil
1 teaspoon salt
¼ teaspoon freshly ground
  black pepper
4 tablespoons flour
3 cups red Burgundy wine
2 cups beef stock
1 tablespoon tomato paste
½ teaspoon crumbled dried
  thyme
1 bay leaf
2 tablespoons chopped fresh
  parsley

Onion Garnish

18 small white onions
  (silverskins)
1½ tablespoons butter
1 tablespoon vegetable oil
1 cup beef stock
1 bouquet garni
¼ teaspoon salt
¼ teaspoon white pepper

Mushroom Garnish

1 pound button mushrooms,
  or large mushrooms
2 tablespoons butter
2 teaspoons oil

With a sharp knife cut the bacon strips into 1-inch crosswise pieces. Place the pieces in a saucepan of water and simmer gently for 10 minutes. Pour off the water and dry the bacon pieces on paper towels. Cut the beef into 2-inch cubes and pat dry with paper towels. Scrape the carrot and peel the

onion. Slice both vegetables. Peel and crush the garlic. Preheat oven to 450°F.

Heat the oil in a large flameproof casserole over moderate heat. Add the bacon pieces and cook for 3 minutes, turning them to brown on both sides. Use a slotted spoon to lift out the bacon to a plate, and set aside. Reheat the fat in the casserole and brown the beef pieces, a few at a time, until seared on all sides. As each batch is done, lift the pieces out and add them to the bacon. Add the carrot and onion slices to the fat and sauté them over moderate heat for 5 minutes. Pour off the fat from the casserole. Return the pieces of beef and bacon, sprinkle with salt and pepper, and sift in the flour. Toss the meat cubes with a wooden spoon to coat them with the flour. Put the uncovered casserole in the center of the oven for 10 minutes. Remove casserole from oven and reduce oven temperature to 325°F.

Pour in the wine and beef stock and add the tomato paste, crushed garlic, thyme and bay leaf. Over moderate heat bring the liquids to the simmering point. Cover the casserole and put it on the lowest shelf of the oven. Cook for about 3 hours, until the beef is tender when pierced with a fork.

Prepare the onion garnish: Peel the onions, leaving them whole. Heat the butter and oil in a saucepan over moderate heat. Add the onions and cook them for 10 mi-

nutes, stirring occasionally so they brown on all sides. Pour in the stock and add the *bouquet garni* and salt and pepper. Cover the pan, reduce the heat, and simmer the onions for 40 minutes, until they are tender but still retain their shape. Remove the *bouquet garni* and set the onions aside.

Prepare the mushroom garnish: Trim mushroom stems and wipe mushrooms with a damp cloth. If they are buttons, leave them whole; if they are large, quarter them through cap and stem. Heat the butter and oil in a skillet over moderate heat. Add the mushrooms and cook, tossing and shaking the pan, for 5 minutes, until they are lightly browned. Set aside.

When the beef is tender, carefully pour all of the juices through a strainer into a large saucepan. Discard the bay leaf. Gently mix the onions and mushrooms into the beef. Skim any fat from the strained sauce. Simmer it over moderate heat for 2 minutes. If it is too thin, boil it rapidly to reduce it. Pour it into the casserole, mix gently, and sprinkle with parsley just before serving from the casserole.

German Pot Roast with Cloves

6 portions

3	pounds top round of beef, in one piece	1	large onion
1	teaspoon dried marjoram	3	carrots
1½	teaspoons salt	1	celery rib
¾	teaspoon black pepper	4	tablespoons butter
1	ounce salt pork	4	tablespoons vegetable oil
8	cloves	1	cup red wine
		1	cup beef stock

Wipe the meat with a damp cloth and place it on a working surface. Combine marjoram with ½ teaspoon salt and ¼ teaspoon pepper on a plate. Cut the salt pork into thin strips and roll each strip in the herb and seasoning mixture. With a sharp knife make small incisions in the beef, or use a larding needle, and insert the salt pork strips. Stud the beef with the cloves. Peel the onion, scrape the carrots, and wash the celery rib. Chop all 3 vegetables.

Melt the butter with the oil in a large flameproof casserole over moderate heat. Add the meat and brown it on all sides. Pour in the wine and stock and bring to a boil. Add the chopped onion, carrots and celery, and remaining salt and pepper. Cover the casserole, reduce heat to low, and simmer for 1¾ hours, until the beef is tender.

Transfer beef to a warmed serving dish and strain the pan juices over it. Serve with potatoes or noodles.

Osso Buco

(Braised Veal Shanks Milanese)

4 portions

4	pieces of veal shin, each about 10 ounces		2	cups canned peeled plum tomatoes
1	tablespoon all-purpose flour			salt and black pepper
1	small onion			
1	small carrot			**Gremolata**
1	celery rib		2	garlic cloves
3	tablespoons olive oil		1	tablespoon grated lemon rind
1	bay leaf		3	tablespoons minced fresh parsley
½	cup dry white wine			

Pat veal pieces dry with paper towels. Sprinkle the flour over the veal and rub it in lightly with the fingers. Peel onion and carrot and wash celery; chop the vegetables into small pieces. Heat the oil in a large heavy pot over moderate heat. Add veal and brown the pieces on all sides. Remove meat with a slotted spoon to a plate. Reduce heat to low; add chopped vegetables and bay leaf to the pot. Cover, and cook for 5 to 6 minutes, stirring occasionally. Pour in the wine and increase the heat so the mixture bubbles briskly and wine is reduced to about 2 tablespoons. Add tomatoes with their liquid. Season the mixture with salt and pepper to taste.

Return the veal pieces to the pot, setting them upright to keep the marrow from falling out. Cover, and simmer for 1½ hours, until veal is tender.

Meanwhile prepare the *gremolata:* Peel the garlic cloves and put through a press. Add lemon rind and parsley and mix together; set aside. With a slotted spoon transfer veal to a warmed serving platter, or to individual plates; keep the veal warm.

Purée vegetables and cooking juices in a food processor or through a food mill; you should have a thick sauce. If sauce is too thin, reduce it by rapid boiling; if it is too thick, thin it with a little veal stock. If necessary, adjust seasonings. Pour the sauce over the veal and sprinkle the *gremolata* on top. Serve with rice.

Veal Fricassee

6 portions

2 pounds boneless veal from the shoulder	2 large onions
salt and pepper	1 large garlic clove
3 tablespoons butter	1 tablespoon flour
2 tablespoons olive oil	4 tablespoons tomato purée
	1½ cups veal stock

Have the veal cut into 1½-inch cubes. Sprinkle with salt and pepper. Heat the butter and oil in a flameproof casserole over moderate heat. Brown the pieces of veal, a few at a time, until they are seared all over.

Peel and chop the onions and garlic. Remove the veal pieces from the casserole as they are browned and set on a plate. When all are done, reduce heat slightly and add onions and garlic to the casserole. Cook, stirring occasionally, until the onion is softened, about 10 minutes. Remove the pot from heat and sprinkle in the flour. Over low heat, cook and stir until the flour is lightly browned and well mixed into the fat and meat juices. Pour in the tomato purée and veal stock and cook, stirring all the while, to deglaze the casserole. Return the veal pieces to the mixture, cover, and cook over low heat for 1½ hours, or less if the veal is fully tender in a shorter time. Skim off any surface fat, check the seasonings, and serve.

Veal Marengo

(Veal Stew with Mushrooms and Onions)

6 portions

3 pounds boned veal from shoulder or leg	½ cup dry white wine
2 teaspoons salt	½ cup veal stock
2 teaspoons black pepper	1 bouquet garni
2 medium-size onions	5 tablespoons tomato purée
2 garlic cloves	1 teaspoon paprika
1 cup canned peeled plum tomatoes	12 small white onions (silverskins)
6 tablespoons butter	12 ounces button mushrooms
4 tablespoons vegetable oil	1 tablespoon beurre manié

Have the veal cut into 2-inch cubes. Place them on a plate and sprinkle with 1 teaspoon salt and 1 teaspoon pepper. Peel and slice the medium-size onions; peel garlic cloves and put through a press into the onions. Chop the tomatoes and keep all the can juices.

Melt 4 tablespoons of the butter with the oil in a large flameproof casserole over moderate heat. Add onions and garlic and cook for 5 to 7 minutes, until onions are soft and translucent but not brown. Stir in the veal cubes and brown them evenly, turning them as they cook for about 10 minutes. Pour in the wine and stock and stir in the *bouquet garni,* the chopped tomatoes and their juices, the tomato purée and paprika. Bring the liquids to a boil, stirring occasionally. Reduce heat to low, cover the casserole, and simmer the stew for 1½ hours.

Peel the small onions, leaving them whole. Wipe the mushrooms, trim base of stems, and leave mushrooms whole. Add onions to the stew and simmer for 30 minutes longer, until the meat is tender.

Meanwhile, melt remaining butter in a skillet and cook the mushrooms, stirring frequently, for 3 minutes. With a slotted spoon transfer mushrooms to a warmed serving dish, large enough to hold all the ingredients. Add the veal cubes and the onions and keep everything warm while finishing the sauce.

Strain the contents of the casserole into a saucepan, pressing hard on the vegetables and flavorings to extract all the juices. Skim any fat or scum from the surface. Bring the liquid to a boil over moderate heat and reduce it by one third. Stir in the *beurre manié,* a bit at a time, stirring constantly, until the sauce has thickened slightly. Pour sauce over the veal and vegetables and serve.

Note: This dish was originally made with chicken; it is said to have been invented for Napoleon after the battle of Marengo. It was usually garnished with crayfish. Either crayfish or shrimps can be added to give additional color and flavor to the dish.

Irish Stew

4 portions

1½	pounds lamb shoulder or leg
3	medium onions
2	pounds small potatoes
	salt and black pepper

1½	cups chicken stock or lamb broth, cold
	chopped fresh parsley
	snipped fresh chives

Cut off and discard all excess fat from the meat. Cut meat into pieces 3 × 2 inches and 1 inch thick, or cut 2-inch cubes. Peel onions and cut into thin slices. Peel potatoes and cut half of them into slices. Put the remaining potatoes in a bowl, cover with cold water, and set aside.

Put the meat into a stewpan, put the sliced onions and potatoes on top, sprinkle generously with salt and black pepper, and pour in the cold stock. Cover tightly. Over low heat bring slowly to a simmer; reduce heat to keep at a simmer and cook for 1 hour.

Drain the whole potatoes and arrange them on top of the stew. Cover and continue simmering for 1 hour longer, until meat and whole potatoes are tender.

Lift out the whole potatoes and arrange them around the outer edge of a serving platter. Lift out the meat and pile it in the center. Skim surface fat from the liquid. Using a wire whisk or a potato masher, beat the mushy sliced potatoes into the cooking liquid to thicken it. Check the seasoning and pour the thickened pan juices over the lamb. Sprinkle with parsley and chives and serve hot.

Italian Lamb Stew with Lemon and Herbs

4 portions

1½	pounds boned lamb from leg or shoulder
2	ounces salt pork
1	small onion
1	tablespoon olive oil
2	tablespoons flour
	salt and white pepper
¼	cup dry white wine

1½	cups lamb broth or chicken stock
1	bay leaf
2	raw egg yolks
1	tablespoon lemon juice
2	tablespoons minced fresh parsley
2	teaspoons minced fresh marjoram

Cut off and discard any gristle from the meat. Wipe the meat with a damp cloth and cut it into 1½-inch cubes. Cut the salt pork into small dice. Peel and chop the onion.

Heat the oil in a flameproof casserole over moderate heat. When sizzling, put in the salt pork and chopped onion. Sauté for 2 minutes, stirring, then add the lamb pieces. Cook for 6 to 8 minutes, stirring frequently, until the onion is beginning to turn golden. Sprinkle in the flour and season with salt and pepper. Cook, stirring, for another 2 minutes. Pour in the wine and let it bubble briskly until almost evaporated. Stir in the broth or stock and add the bay leaf. Bring to a boil, then reduce heat to low. Cover the casserole and simmer the stew for 45 minutes, until the pieces of meat are tender when pierced with a fork. Stir occasionally.

Remove casserole from heat and skim off surplus fat. If a lot of the liquid has evaporated, add enough extra broth or stock, hot, to have 1½ cups. Check the seasoning and remove the bay leaf. When ready to serve, beat together in a bowl the raw egg yolks, lemon juice, parsley and marjoram. Stir in 2 tablespoons of the hot broth from the lamb to warm the eggs. Stirring all the time, pour this mixture into the casserole and cook over low heat until the egg has thickened the sauce slightly. Do not let the sauce boil after adding the egg mixture or it will curdle. Serve at once.

Braised Lamb Shanks

6 portions

3	lamb shanks, 1 pound each
1	large onion
10	plum tomatoes, or 1½ cups canned peeled plum tomatoes
1	tablespoon olive oil

1	cup red wine
2	teaspoons grated orange rind
1	teaspoon ground cuminseed
	salt
	chopped parsley

Have the butcher crack the shanks so it will be easy to fit them in a casserole. Preheat oven to 375°F. Arrange shanks in a casserole only slightly larger than the meat, and add no other ingredients. Cover, and roast them in the oven for 1 hour. (This takes the place of browning.) Remove shanks to a plate and pour off all the fat; blot the casserole with paper towels to remove the last drops. Return shanks to the casserole. (This much can be done a day ahead; in that case, cool the lamb and refrigerate until ready to proceed. Let casserole and lamb return to room temperature before continuing.)

Peel and mince the onion. Blanch and peel the tomatoes and chop them; discard as many seeds as possible. Heat the oil in a skillet and cook onion until golden in color and very soft. Add chopped tomatoes and cook for 10 minutes, stirring. Stir in the wine, orange rind, cuminseed and 1 teaspoon salt.

Reduce oven heat to 350°F. Remove the meat from the shank bones; keep the bones. Cut meat into large chunks. Return meat and bones to the casserole and pour in the onion mixture. Cover, return casserole to the oven, and braise for 1 hour.

Remove and discard the bones. Taste, and add more salt if needed. Gently mix the ingredients and sprinkle with parsley. Serve from the casserole.

Cooked dried beans, especially green flageolets or Great Northern beans, are an excellent accompaniment to this dish. The beans can be reheated in the casserole to become very flavorful; it may be necessary to add a little stock or water as the beans will absorb most of the pan juices.

Greek Lamb Stew

6 portions

2 pounds lean lamb, from shoulder or leg
2 pounds small new potatoes
8 ounces small white onions (silverskins)
2 cups canned peeled tomatoes
½ cup olive oil
6 ounces tomato purée

¾ cup dry red wine
2 tablespoons vinegar
2 teaspoons salt
3 bay leaves
1 tablespoon lemon juice
3 ounces blanched almonds (½ cup)
6 ounces feta cheese

Have the lamb cut into 2-inch cubes. Scrub and halve the potatoes; do not peel them. Peel the onions and leave them whole. Drain and chop the tomatoes. Heat the olive oil in a deep flameproof casserole over moderate heat. Add the lamb pieces and cook for 5 minutes, until the pieces are lightly browned on all sides. Brown part at a time if the pot does not hold them all in a single layer. With a slotted spoon transfer the pieces to a plate. Add the potatoes and onions to the casserole and cook them for 8 minutes, turning them now and then, until the onions are lightly browned.

Pour the tomatoes, tomato purée, red wine and vinegar into a saucepan and stir in the salt; bring the mixture to a boil, stirring frequently. Remove pan from heat and set the tomato sauce aside.

When the onions are browned, return the lamb pieces to the casserole and stir in the tomato sauce. Add the bay leaves. Reduce heat to low, cover the casserole, and simmer the stew, stirring now and then, for 1½ hours, until lamb is very tender.

Stir in the lemon juice and almonds and crumble the cheese on top of the stew. Set again over heat for 5 to 8 minutes, until the cheese has melted. Transfer the stew to a warmed serving dish and serve at once.

Navarin Printanier
(French Lamb Stew with Spring Vegetables)

6 portions

1 pound boned shoulder of lamb	2 tablespoons tomato purée
1½ pounds breast of lamb	1 garlic clove
2 tablespoons oil	1 bouquet garni
2 teaspoons granulated sugar	12 small white onions (silverskins)
1½ tablespoons flour	1 pound small new potatoes
salt and pepper	6 to 10 small new carrots
2 cups chicken stock or lamb broth	1 pound fresh peas in shells

Wipe the meat with a damp cloth. Remove bones from the breast meat and set them aside. Trim off excess fat and skin. Cut all the meat into 1½-inch cubes and blot dry on paper towels. Preheat oven to 300°F.

Pour the oil into a flameproof casserole large enough to hold the meat and all the vegetables, about 3-quart size. Heat the oil over moderate heat. When the oil is almost smoking, put in the meat, a few pieces at a time, in a single layer, and brown them quickly to sear all sides. Continue until all the pieces are browned. Pour off the fat, and combine all the meat in the casserole. Reduce heat slightly and sprinkle the sugar over the meat. Cook and stir until the sugar is lightly caramelized. Sprinkle in the flour and a generous amount of salt and pepper, and stir, still over low heat, for 2 or 3 minutes, until the flour is light brown. Heat the stock or broth and mix in the tomato purée. Pour the liquid into the casserole and bring to a simmer, still stirring. Peel the garlic and put through a press into the meat. Add the *bouquet garni* and place the reserved lamb bones on top of the meat. Cover casserole and cook in the oven for 1 hour.

Prepare the spring vegetables: Peel the onions; leave them whole. Scrape or scrub the potatoes and carrots; leave them whole. Shell the peas.

Remove casserole from the oven and lift off the bones. Skim excess fat from the surface. Add onions and carrots and push them down into the stew liquid. Cover and cook in the oven for another 30 minutes. Add potatoes and peas and cook for 15 minutes longer, until potatoes are tender and meat done to your taste. Lift out and discard the *bouquet garni*. If there is fat on the surface, skim it off. Check the seasoning. Serve from the casserole.

Variations: For a winter *navarin,* omit the spring vegetables and use onions and soaked dried shell beans, about 8 ounces dry weight. Chopped tomatoes can be added, with some of the juice serving in place of part of the stock or broth.

Lamb and Kidney Hotpot

4 portions

1½ pounds lamb rib chops	salt and black pepper
4 lambs' kidneys	2 tablespoons butter
8 ounces onions	1 cup chicken stock or lamb broth
1½ pounds potatoes	

Preheat oven to 325°F. Trim the pieces of meat of any surplus fat and rinse off any splinters of bone (sometimes the bones splinter when the butcher is cutting the ribs apart). Peel away the fat and skin surrounding the kidneys. Cut out the hard center portion. Split each kidney into halves through the center. Peel the onions and cut into thin slices. Peel the potatoes and cut each one into 6 thick slices. Starting with a layer of potatoes, fill a hotpot or deep casserole with alternate layers of potato, lamb, kidney and onion. Season each layer lightly. Top with a layer of potato slices, arranging them so they overlap like roof tiles to cover the meat completely. Dot the potatoes with small bits of butter. Pour in the stock at the edge of the casserole. Cover tightly and set in the center of the oven. Braise for 1½ hours, reducing heat if the stew cooks too fast. Uncover the hotpot and cook for 30 minutes longer to allow the potatoes to brown. Serve from the pot.

Braised Pork with Sour-Cream and Caraway Sauce

4 to 6 portions

4 tablespoons butter	1 teaspoon salt
2 tablespoons vegetable oil	½ teaspoon black pepper
3 pounds boned loin of pork, rolled and tied	2 tablespoons beurre manié
2 large onions	1 cup dairy sour cream
1 tablespoon paprika	1 tablespoon snipped fresh chives
1 cup dry white wine	1 tablespoon caraway seeds
¾ cup chicken stock	

Preheat oven to 350°F. Melt the butter with the oil in a large flameproof casserole over moderate heat. Add the rolled pork and brown it on all sides. Remove pork to a plate. Peel and chop the onions and cook them in the fat remaining in the casserole for 6 to 8 minutes, until golden brown. Remove casserole from heat and stir in the paprika. Pour in the wine and stock and add salt and pepper. Return casserole to heat and bring to a boil, stirring constantly. Return the pork to the casserole, cover, and put the pot in the oven. Braise for about 1½ hours, until pork is well cooked but not dried out.

Transfer pork to a warmed serving dish and keep it hot while you make the sauce. Strain the braising juices into a saucepan. Bring to a boil and boil rapidly for about 4 minutes, until the liquid is reduced by one quarter. Reduce heat to low and stir in the *beurre manié,* small bits at a time. Continue stirring until the sauce is smooth and thickened. Stir in the sour cream, chives and caraway seeds. Heat gently, stirring occasionally, until the sauce is hot. Do not let it boil after adding the sour cream, or the cream will separate. Pour the sauce into a warmed sauceboat and serve it with the pork.

Pork, Cabbage and Cider Casserole

6 portions

2 pounds lean fresh pork, from shoulder, loin or leg	1 cup cider
1 teaspoon oil	1 teaspoon salt
4 medium-size onions	freshly ground black pepper
2 celery ribs	12 juniper berries
1 large garlic clove	2 tablespoons chopped fresh parsley
1 pound white cabbage	1 cup crisp fried croutons
2 tablespoons flour	

Preheat oven to 300°F. Wipe the meat with a damp cloth. Remove all the bones; set these aside, they will be needed later. Cut the meat into 1½-inch cubes. Heat the oil in a skillet over moderate heat. When hot, sauté half of the meat, stirring frequently, until fat is released from the pork and the meat begins to turn golden. Do not overcook at this stage or the pork will become tough on the outside. With a slotted spoon, transfer the meat to a large casserole, about 3-quart capacity. Continue with the rest of the meat. Remove skillet from heat.

Peel and slice the onions. Wash and slice the celery. Peel and crush the garlic. Wash, drain, and shred the cabbage. Return skillet to low heat and cook onions and celery in the fat released by the pork until onions are beginning to soften, about 10 minutes. Add garlic and fry for another minute. Sprinkle the flour over the vegetables and cook, stirring, for 2 minutes to brown the flour lightly. Stir in the cider and bring to a boil. Pour the contents of the skillet into the casserole. Add the shredded cabbage, the salt, and a generous sprinkling of pepper. Crush the juniper berries in a mortar and add them. Stir to mix everything thoroughly. Lay the reserved pork bones on top. Bring the liquid to a simmer over low heat. Cover tightly and place in the center of the oven. Cook for 1½ hours, or until the pork is tender when pierced with a fork. Check the cooking occasionally and adjust the oven temperature if necessary to keep the stew at a simmer.

Remove the bones and check the seasoning. Stir in the parsley. Sprinkle the croutons on top and serve from the casserole.

Pork with Orange Sauce

6 to 8 portions

4½	pounds fresh pork shoulder
½	cup white stock
1	cup dry white wine
3	oranges

Dry Marinade

3	garlic cloves
1	teaspoon coarse salt

3	tablespoons oil
1	tablespoon chopped fresh parsley
1	teaspoon minced fresh marjoram
2	sprigs of rosemary, crushed
½	teaspoon freshly ground black pepper

Remove any rind and as much fat as possible from the pork. Peel the garlic and crush with the coarse salt. Mix with the oil, parsley, marjoram, rosemary and black pepper. Rub the marinade mixture all over the pork. Put the meat in a covered dish in the refrigerator for at least 4 hours, or overnight, to absorb the flavors.

Preheat oven to 300°F. Scrape the herbs off the meat with the blunt side of a knife. Brown the meat in a flameproof casserole over high heat. The pork will be oily from the marinade, but you may need to add a little extra oil. When the meat is browned on all sides, pour in the stock, wine and the juice of 1 orange. Bring liquids to a boil. Cover tightly. Transfer casserole to the oven and braise for 2 to 2½ hours, until pork is fully cooked.

Remove pork from the casserole and keep it warm. Skim any fat from the pan juices. Peel remaining 2 oranges and separate into segments. Poach the segments in the pan juices just long enough to warm them through. Slice the pork and arrange on a hot serving dish. Surround with the orange segments. Strain the pan juices into a sauceboat and serve with the meat.

Part Three
BASIC ITALIAN PASTA

"Whenever I think of pasta I think of my godfather, Tommaso, who returned to his native Abruzzi in Italy after he retired. He died a few months ago, at eighty-six," writes artist Edward Giobbi. "Tommaso ate macaroni in one form or another every day. He bought his pasta imported from Italy in 25-pound crates . . . Tommaso would eat two pounds of pasta at a sitting, yet he was never overweight and he never went to a doctor or a dentist. He had all his teeth when he died" *(Italian Family Cooking)*.

Pasta, in one form or another, has been a popular food for centuries, especially in Italy. Although Marco Polo has often been credited with introducing pasta to Italy on his return from China, this is only one more in the long list of misconceptions about this much beloved but misunderstood food.

No one knows exactly how long Italians have been eating pasta, but pasta dishes were flourishing and well established by the thirteenth century, certainly long before the expeditions of Marco Polo. By the end of the Middle Ages, foreigners were poking fun at Italy as a nation of macaroni-eaters and it seems that from time to time, Italians themselves worried about overindulging in their national culinary passion. Elizabeth David writes that "in the sixteenth century a Genoese doctor denounced the abuse of *pasta*. Toward the end of the eighteenth century a campaign was instituted against the consumption of excessive quantities of macaroni. Innumerable volumes from the hands of eminent scientists and men of letters proved unavailing" *(Italian Food)*. As did the diatribe of the Italian futurist poet Marinetti in 1930, in which he accused pasta of being "heavy, brutalizing, and gross," at the same time that it "induces scepticism, sloth and pessimism."

Whether due to scepticism, stubbornness or simple disbelief, Italians went on eating pasta with no apparent detriment to health or character. To this day there exists a fount of folklore about the many benefits of pasta, both as an antidote to illness and as a factor in longevity as well.

Americans ate quantities of noodles, macaroni and spaghetti, long before the word *pasta* became fashionable. Unfortunately, for many years, the pleasure people derived from eating this delicious food was marred by pangs of guilt because of yet another misconception. Pasta, people were told, along with other carbohydrates like bread, potatoes, rice, would make them fat. Happily for everyone, this is not true.

Until quite recently the role of carbohydrates in nutrition had not been fully understood, so for years people who wanted to lose weight were told to eat their steak and put aside the pasta or potatoes. Today we've come full circle and we know that we would all be healthier and slimmer too if we would eat a plate of pasta and only just a little bit of meat.

In many ways, pasta is an ideal food for modern living. It is low in fat and a good source of proteins and complex carbohydrates. According to the National Macaroni Institute, 2 ounces of uncooked macaroni contain only 200 calories.

There are two fundamental types of Italian pasta. One is made of water and durum-wheat semolina, the finely ground heart of the kernels of a particularly gluten-rich strain of wheat. This is the usual commercial *pasta secca,* or dry pasta, mechanically cut or extruded through dies to form dozens of different shapes and sold in packaged form. Because of the gluten content of the wheat, it will cook when properly handled to a slightly firm, wonderfully toothsome consistency. This *al dente* (to the tooth) effect can be most fully appreciated in the factory pasta from the Abruzzi and regions to the south.

Pasta fresca or *pasta all'uovo* (fresh pasta, egg pasta) is more of a northern specialty, usually made from "softer" (less glutinous) varieties of wheat. The liquid used is most often egg, which further tenderizes the dough. *Pasta all'uovo* is generally homemade rather than factory-made, and cannot be cooked to the same *al dente* resilience as durum-wheat pasta; it is basically a noodle dough, and it cooks like noodles. Though it too can be forced through dies, more often it is simply cut into ribbons or other flat shapes. It is the preferred form of pasta for many if not most uses in the north of Italy; *pasta secca* is the favorite in the south. Both are often tinted green by the addition of chopped spinach.

The *pasta secca* that we can buy comes in an enormous variety of shapes and sizes. It can be as thin as a strand of hair or as thick as your thumb, it can be flat like *linguine* and *fettuccine,* spiraled and grooved like *rigatoni,* or shaped like seashells, *conchiglie.*

The basic shape of the pasta usually determines how it is cooked and served. The tiniest pasta shapes—*acini di pepe, anelli, orzo, funghini* (to name just a few)—would be drowned in most sauces and are usually cooked and served *in brodo,* in a clear broth.

Very large or sturdy shapes that will not soften as fast in cooking are often briefly cooked and used for different versions of *pasta al forno* (baked pasta, usually with a rich sauce). Most others become *pasta asciutta,* or literally "dried-off pasta," boiled in water and drained before saucing. Sauces do not cling to the smoother pasta shapes as well as to ridged or hollow forms. In Italy, the matching of pasta shape to sauce is an important consideration. With smooth, thin pasta it is more appropriate to serve simple dressings based on oil or butter or, at most, fresh light-textured sauces. Rich, heavy-textured sauces do well with larger pasta or intricate shapes that can capture little mouthfuls of sauce in their recesses.

For homemade egg pasta, the traditional forms include some flat shapes and some that are rolled around a filling; *lasagne, cannelloni, ravioli* and *tortellini* are some of the many types of pasta that can be made at home with *pasta all'uovo.* The smaller stuffed pasta types are often served in broth, the large ones usually baked with sauces.

Some kind of pasta, dried or fresh, with and without eggs, and using various other flours, is eaten throughout most of Europe and almost everywhere in Asia and the Middle East.

In Germany and Austria pasta forms part of the vast repertoire of *Suppeneinlage,* or "things to put in soups," a category that includes everything from noodles to dumplings.

In various parts of the Austro-Hungarian Empire noodles also came to be a dessert. Ordinary buttered noodles can simply be sprinkled with poppy seeds and sugar, or the dough itself can be sweetened. The Eastern European Jews who came to America brought with them *lokshen kugel,* a popular variant on the idea in which noodles are baked in a sweet pudding enriched with pot cheese and raisins. They also brought their own version of small stuffed pasta for soups: *kreplach,* a traditional accompaniment for chicken soup.

Rishta are the Middle Eastern version of fresh egg noodles, served like Italian *pasta all'uovo* either *asciutta* (drained, to be covered with a savory sauce) or *al forno* (baked with layers of sauce.) To the north and east, egg noodles are found in the Central Asian republics of the USSR, while Siberia has its own version of stuffed egg pasta: *pelmeny,* similar to tiny meat-stuffed ravioli.

The Chinese noodle repertoire outdoes the Italian in at least one respect: not only does it use wheat-flour doughs (both with and without eggs), but it has other varieties based on such ingredients as rice flour and mung bean starch (the source of the transparent, slippery "cellophane noodles"). Chinese egg noodles made of wheat flour are the most popular and versatile of the family. They are a staple food in the north, a beloved snack in the south. China also rivals Italy in its inventiveness with small and stuffed dough shapes, of which the most familiar to Americans are wontons and *chiao-tze,* usually called "dumplings."

Japan, along with many kinds of noodles made from wheat, also has buckwheat flour noodles called *soba,* many transparent noodles, noodles made with seaweed and sometimes with green tea.

People eat noodles everywhere and various countries have different rules of etiquette about the proper way to eat them. In Japan, for example, it is considered proper and desirable to make a breathy, slurping sound while eating noodles that are hot, the idea being that you are cooling them while they are en route to your mouth. And it may still come as a rude surprise to some that Italians do not use a spoon to help them eat spaghetti. Christopher Morley may have made the best observation of all when he said, "No man is lonely while eating spaghetti—it requires too much attention. . . ."

PASTA

There are so many varieties of pasta available today that you can literally serve a different kind of pasta every day for a year and not exhaust the possibilities. When you consider the many ways that pasta can be served: in soups; in delicate, small portions to begin a meal; alongside any meat, poultry, fish or seafood; or as a hearty main course with an astonishing variety of sauces; you can appreciate just why this versatile and most accommodating food has grown so popular.

Some Pasta Facts

• Dried pasta (pasta secca) is the most popular and widely available type. It is made of a simple paste of semolina flour mixed with water. The semolina grains are made by milling the inner part of the kernels of a particularly hard wheat called durum wheat, grown around the Mediterranean and in North America. Durum wheat flour contains a lot of protein in the form of gluten which makes it "strong" like bread flour, so that it keeps its shape, texture and flavor when cooked, even without eggs to hold it together. The dough is pushed through nozzles of various shapes, and is then dried carefully and evenly, so that it is hard. Dried pasta keeps for months, provided it is stored correctly either in a pasta jar or by sealing the packet after opening.
• Fresh pasta (pasta fresca) is often made from hard wheat as well, but it usually includes eggs along with water. Until quite recently fresh pasta could only be had by making it at home, but now many specialty and gourmet shops make up batches of fresh pasta to sell on a daily basis. Because fresh pasta freezes well, it can often be found in the frozen food section of many

stores. Store fresh pasta in the refrigerator until ready to use.
• Colored pasta, usually flavored with spinach or tomatoes, has become popular in recent years and can be found dried as well as fresh.
• Whole-grain pasta, made with whole-wheat flour, rye flour and buckwheat flour, is darker in color and denser in texture than other kinds of pasta. It is popular with vegetarians and health-food fans and can most easily be found in health-food stores and in selected supermarkets.

Pasta Shapes

Italy has given us the largest and most imaginative variety of shapes and sizes. The following is only a small sampling of the many kinds of pasta that can be found on supermarket shelves and in specialty stores. Not included here are the varieties of filled pasta (ravioli, tortellini, etc.) as they will be treated in a future volume.

Acini di Pepe. Tiny pasta "peppercorns," most often used in soups, especially in clear meat or chicken broth.

Alphabets. Not exactly Italian, but so popular with children that they should not be left out. Serve in alphabet soup, of course.

Anelli and Anellini. Thin-sliced tubes or rings. Traditionally served in soup.

Bucatini. Sometimes called *perciatelli* ("pierced"); thin, tubular pasta; *bucatini* are slightly thinner than spaghetti, *perciatelli* are slightly thicker than spaghetti. Good with all tomato sauces.

Cannelle and Cannellini. "Small reeds" and "tiny reeds," these are hollow and related to the much larger *cannelloni* (to be discussed in a future volume on *Stuffed Pasta*). Good with all tomato sauces and hearty meat sauces.

Capelli d'Angelo and Capellini. Pasta that is as fine as "angel's hair." Dried, it is often sold rolled up in a nest, and it is sometimes available

Pasta Shapes

Alphabets

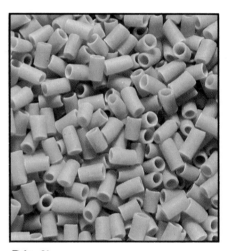
Ditali

freshly made. It is usually served in a clear beef broth with grated Parmesan cheese, or as a first course in a delicate cream and butter sauce.

Cavatapi. Small pasta elbow twists that look like corkscrews. Particularly good with meat sauces and any other sauces that need a bit of mopping up.

Cavatelli. A pretty, shell-shaped pasta with a rippled surface. Good with all kinds of hearty sauces.

Conchiglie (also Maruzze). Shell-shaped pasta with a hollow, made in many sizes. The name means

Capelli d'Angelo

Conchiglie

Cravatte

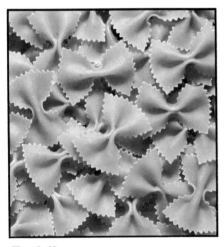

Farfalle

Fettuccine

Fusilli

"conch" after the shell that it resembles. The smaller ones are good with any hearty sauce because the cavity is good for catching bits of meat and vegetables. The larger shells are often stuffed and baked.

Conchigliette. These are amusing tiny shells to serve in soups, both clear and hearty.

Cravatte. These pasta "bowties" are tied like ribbons. They're good with simple butter and cheese sauces as well as any light tomato sauce.

Creste di Galli. Medium-size elbow-shaped pasta with a ruffled crest

that resembles a "cockscomb." Good with all hearty sauces.

Ditali and Ditalini. Small hollow macaroni cut into very short lengths. The name means "thimbles." Serve in soups, especially minestrone and other hearty vegetable soups.

Farfalle. "Butterflies" that look like bows. Also *farfalline,* "tiny butterflies," and *farfalloni,* "big butterflies."

Fedelini. Very thin spaghetti, usually thinner than *vermicelli,* these "faithful ones" are often sold in clusters or nests. Good with delicate sauces and in soup.

Fettuccine. These "small ribbons" are among the most popular of all Italian noodles. They are normally about ¼ inch wide and are often available fresh, made with eggs. Serve with creamy cheese sauce (as in *Fettuccine Alfredo*) or with delicate seafood sauces.

Fusilli. Spaghetti pieces twisted into spirals. Good with thick, creamy sauces.

Lasagne. Very wide strips of pasta, sometimes sold fresh and made with eggs, sometimes flavored with spinach. These are usually layered in casseroles.

Linguine. The name means "little tongues." This thick, narrow type is most popular with clam sauce, but good with vegetable sauces or pesto.

Maccheroni. (Macaroni) A general term for tubular pasta, including all elbows and *ziti.* Macaroni is often a hearty dish baked in casserole.

Maruzze. These "seashells" come in many sizes. Also see *conchiglie.*

Mostaccioli. Whimsically titled "small mustaches," these are pasta tubes with diagonally cut ends. Good with creamy sauces.

Orzo. Although the name means "barley," this tiny pasta looks like rice. Serve in soup or in place of rice. Toss with butter and grated Parmesan.

Penne. "Pens" or "quills," this pasta is similar to *mostaccioli.*

Rigatoni. Ridged tubes good for scooping up sauce. Usually served as a main course with a hearty sauce, or in gratin dishes.

Rotelle. These "small wheels" can be served with hearty tomato and meat sauces.

Spaghetti. Literally "strings," this most popular of all pasta types comes in a variety of thicknesses and lengths.

Stellini. "Little stars" make a big hit in soups.

Tagliatelle. A little wider than *fettuccine,* these are also often available fresh and sometimes in a spinach-flavored green color. This noodle is most often served with meat sauce, especially the famous *Bolognese.*

Pasta Shapes (continued)

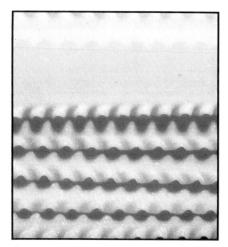

Lasagne

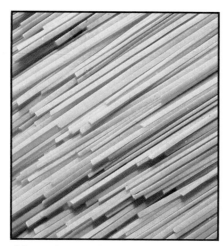

Linguine

**Maccheroni
(Elbow Macaroni)**

Rigatoni

Rotelle

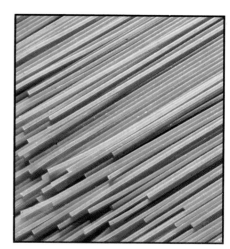

Spaghetti

Tubettini. Tiny tubes usually served in soup.

Vermicelli. These "little worms" are a very thin spaghetti; sometimes sold in nest form.

Ziti. The name of this tubular pasta means "bridegrooms" and it is served with many kinds of hearty sauces and baked in casseroles.

Choosing Pasta Shapes

The tiny pasta shapes—alphabets, acini di pepe, anellini, conchigliette, ditalini, farfalline, stellini and tubettini—are all too small to hold up well in a sauce. These baby shapes (along with the fine, threadlike capellini) are used in soups and broths. The charming shapes have great appeal in very clear broths, and they add substance to many vegetable soups. Some tiny pasta shapes, particularly *orzo,* can be served as a delicious substitute for rice or any other grains. This cooked pasta should be tossed with butter and grated Parmesan cheese, and served immediately.

The long smooth types of pasta, such as all the types of spaghetti, linguine and fettuccine, are at their best when served with sauces that have a clinging, creamy texture.

The shaped pasta types—shells, fusilli, rotelle, all the kinds of macaroni—work well with meat sauces. Their stubby shapes, hollows, crevices, etc., help capture bits of meat and sauce.

These are only guidelines. Feel free to substitute and experiment to find your own favorite combinations of shapes and texture.

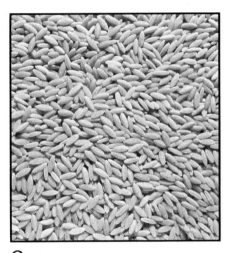

Orzo

Penne

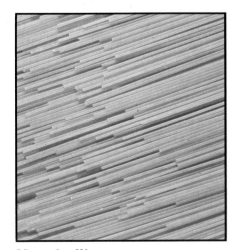

Vermicelli

Ziti

How to Cook Pasta

Equipment. You will need a pot large enough to hold at least 6 quarts of water; a long wooden fork; a colander to drain the pasta; a large, heated bowl in which to toss the pasta with the sauce.

How Much Water? For 1 pound of pasta you should boil 6 quarts of water. If you are cooking smaller amounts of pasta, say ½ pound, do *not* decrease the water by half. Four quarts is good. If you are cooking more than 1 pound of pasta, use 2 pots.

Cooking the Pasta. Add salt when water boils—1 to 2 tablespoons per 6 quarts of water. (Or omit salt if it is not permitted in your diet.) Add the pasta all at once. If you are cooking long pasta, i.e., spaghetti, press it in the middle with a wooden fork until it bends and is completely submerged in the water. Cover the pot, but only until water returns to the boil. Remove cover and cook at a rapid boil until done. Stir the pasta once or twice with the wooden fork to separate the pieces.

Saucing and Serving Pasta. The sauce that you are using should always be ready and waiting for the pasta. Add sauce, butter, and cheese if called for, and mix quickly to blend and distribute the sauce. Serve pasta immediately.

Boiling Pasta

1 pound dry pasta
2 tablespoons salt
2 tablespoons butter or
    olive oil

• Cooking times are indicated on every package of commercially produced pasta, but personal taste combined with common sense will be a more accurate guide.

• To test whether the pasta is ready:

• Two minutes before the pasta should be done, take out a strand with a fork or a round shape with a slotted spoon. Taste it.

• The pasta is ready as soon as it has lost its floury taste, but is still firm to bite—what Italians call *al dente.* Do not cook pasta until it is soft or mushy.

• If the pasta is not yet ready when you taste it, taste another strand or shape every minute or so until it is done.

• As soon as the pasta is ready, drain it into a large colander or sieve. Give the colander a few good shakes to get rid of all the water and remove the pasta to a heated serving bowl.

1 Bring 6 quarts of water to a rolling boil in a large pot. When water is boiling, add the salt.

2 Add pasta to the water. Do not break long strands.

5 Drop bundles into boiling water, wait 1 minute, then stir to separate.

6 Cook pasta uncovered at a steady boil, stirring once or twice, until tender to your taste.

Sauces for Pasta

There are literally hundreds of sauces for pasta, ranging from simple herb and oil to the well-known, meaty Bolognese. Usually the simple cheese or cream sauces are served when pasta is used as a first course and the more complicated, meaty sauces when it is used as a main course. Some of the sauces are so simple that they are hardly a sauce at all.

Ingredients

• Sweet (unsalted) butter has freshest, purest flavor and is always the preferred choice for pasta.

• Use the best imported olive oil (preferably Italian) that you can afford.

• Parmesan cheese is a crucial flavor element in many pasta dishes. For best results buy the best-quality, aged Parmesan imported from Italy. Avoid cheese that is already grated. Buy the

cheese in one piece and grate it just before adding to pasta.

• Pecorino cheese, also imported from Italy, has a sharper, stronger taste. This too is better bought by the chunk and grated freshly for each use. It may be mixed half and half with Parmesan for certain pasta dishes.

• Use fresh herbs whenever possible. Fresh basil is essential for pesto, a basil and garlic sauce, and delicious in many other sauces. Parsley is frequent-

3 As pasta softens, ends will bend; push down the strands. When all pasta is in the pot, stir.

4 Small shapes may be dropped into the water a few at a time. Stir after each addition to prevent sticking.

7 Drain cooked pasta in a large colander.

8 Return pasta to the pot or to a warmed serving bowl and toss with butter or oil.

ly called for and it is important to note that the flat-leafed Italian variety has more flavor and aroma than the curly-leafed variety.

• Pepper and nutmeg are the spices most often used. Both have much better flavor when they are freshly grated.

Simple Sauces, Quickly Made

Some of the most delicious sauces for pasta take literally only minutes to pre-pare. Among these sauces are the following:

Butter and Parmesan Cheese. Pasta served this way is only as good as the ingredients used. Toss with butter and add grated Parmesan cheese. Serve in warmed plates.

With the addition of heavy cream this becomes *Fettuccine Alfredo.*

Oil and Garlic. This is one of the best loved of all sauces for pasta. Mince several garlic cloves and sauté gently in good olive oil until golden brown. Toss with pasta and garnish with minced fresh parsley.

Vegetables and Cheese. Cut any tender vegetables into slices or chunks and sauté quickly in butter and oil. Toss with pasta and top with cheese. Good choices are asparagus, broccoli, cauliflower and zucchini.

Tomato Sauce. This large category includes very light sauces made in minutes as well as sauces that simmer for an hour or so. Tomato sauces can be creamy and delicate as well as spicy and robust.

Uncooked Tomato Sauce. Make this sauce in the height of summer when luscious vine-ripened tomatoes are in great abundance. Fresh basil is a favorite flavoring herb.

Fresh Tomato Sauce. Another sauce to make when vine-ripened tomatoes are in season. This sauce has a delicate sweet taste and is sometimes enriched with heavy cream.

Marinara Sauce. This tangy, fresh-tasting sauce is spiked with garlic and herbs. When fresh tomatoes are not available, it can be made with good-quality canned tomatoes.

All-Purpose Tomato Sauce. A basic tomato sauce, made with canned tomatoes and flavored with aromatic vegetables. It can be thickened with tomato paste. Any number of ingredients can be added to transform this basic sauce; bacon, chicken livers, mushrooms, or seafood, are just a few of the many possibilities.

Hearty Sauces

There are many hearty sauces based on meat, poultry and seafood that combine with pasta to make delicious main-course meals. One of the most popular of these is the Bolognese Sauce, which combines beef, chicken livers and bits of bacon or ham in a hearty tomato sauce.

Other main-course sauces can be made with savory Italian sausages, mushrooms, all sorts of seafood, and game. Some famous Italian sauces are based on hare or rabbit, and quail is another favorite.

Bolognese Sauce

3½ to 4 cups sauce

6   strips of smoked bacon
1   medium-size onion
1   medium-size carrot
1   celery rib
8   ounces chopped lean beef
4   ounces chicken livers
2   tablespoons butter
1   tablespoon tomato paste
1   cup white wine
1   cup beef stock
    salt and black pepper

1 Remove any rind from bacon and cut strips into small pieces. Peel and mince the onion.

2 Scrub and chop carrot and celery. Break up the chopped beef. Wash and dry chicken livers.

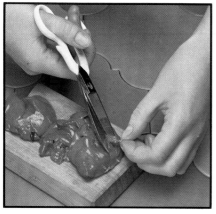

3 Discard any greenish parts from the livers, then chop them into small pieces.

4 Heat the butter in a heavy saucepan over moderate heat. Cook bacon pieces until just brown.

5 Add onion, carrot and celery. Cook until onion is tender and turning brown. Mix in the chopped beef.

6 Stir the beef until it browns all over. Add chicken livers and cook for 3 minutes longer.

7 Mix in the tomato paste. Pour in the wine and stock and bring to a boil.

8 Reduce heat and simmer, covered, for 30 minutes. Season to taste.

Tomato Sauce

2½ to 3 cups sauce

2½ pounds fresh ripe
    tomatoes
½ garlic clove
1 small onion
1 carrot

1 celery rib
    salt and black pepper
    pinch of sugar
1 tablespoon minced fresh
    basil

Blanch, peel and chop the tomatoes; put them in a large heavy saucepan. Peel garlic and put through a press into the tomatoes. Peel the onion, scrub and scrape the carrot, and wash the celery. Chop all these vegetables and add to the tomatoes. Season lightly with salt and pepper and add the pinch of sugar. Do not add water; the tomatoes supply enough liquid. Bring to the boiling point, then lower the heat so the liquid barely simmers. Cover the pan and cook, stirring frequently, for 1 hour.

Put the sauce through a coarse sieve or a food mill into a clean saucepan. Check the seasoning. When ready to serve the sauce, reheat it, or simmer to reduce and thicken it, before using it. Sprinkle basil over the sauce.

Variations: Other herbs can be used to flavor this sauce. Grated cheese can be stirred in. The longer the sauce is cooked, the thicker it will be and the less sauce you will have.

Marinara Sauce

2½ to 3 cups sauce

2	pounds ripe plum tomatoes	½	cup chopped fresh parsley
3	garlic cloves	½	teaspoon crumbled dried orégano
2	small onions	1	teaspoon salt
¼	cup olive oil		black pepper

Blanch and peel tomatoes and chop them. Peel garlic cloves. Peel and chop onions. Heat the oil in a large skillet. Push garlic through a press into the oil and sauté, stirring, until garlic is lightly colored. Add onions and sauté until they are soft. Pour in chopped tomatoes and add ¼ cup of the parsley, the orégano and the salt. Stir to mix well, then simmer for about 30 minutes. Add pepper to taste and stir in the rest of the parsley. Serve at once on freshly cooked pasta.

When ripe tomatoes are not in the market, use 3½ cups canned peeled plum tomatoes. This sauce can be puréed if you like, but it should be a simple, quickly prepared sauce without frills. The sauce can be flavored with basil or bay leaf. It can be cooked longer to make a more concentrated sauce.

Walnut Sauce

about 1 cup

4	ounces shelled walnuts	1	tablespoon olive oil
6	sprigs of fresh marjoram		salt and black pepper
1	bunch of fresh parsley		fresh soft white bread crumbs (optional)
½	cup heavy cream		

Put the walnuts in a heatproof bowl and cover with boiling water. Let them stand for about 2 minutes, then drain and peel off as much of the skins as possible. Pick the leaves from the marjoram sprigs and the parsley stems. Put the walnuts in a food processor fitted with the steel blade and grate walnuts into small crumbs. Leave walnuts in the bowl and add the marjoram and parsley leaves. Process again until you have a thick smooth paste. Pour the cream through the feed

tube, as if making a mayonnaise, until you have a soft, pale green paste. Scrape the sauce into a bowl. Mix in the oil and season to taste. If the sauce is too thin, add some of the bread crumbs, 1 tablespoon at a time, until the texture is just right. If sauce is too thick, add a little more cream to thin it to the right consistency.

An excellent sauce for tagliatelle; also good on fish.

Red Clam Sauce (with canned clams)

3 cups sauce

2	garlic cloves	½	teaspoon white pepper
1	small onion	½	teaspoon dried basil
1	tablespoon capers	2	cups canned minced clams
2	cups canned peeled plum tomatoes	1	tablespoon chopped fresh parsley
3	tablespoons olive oil		lemon juice

Peel the garlic cloves and drop them into the bowl of a food processor fitted with the steel blade. Peel the onion, cut into small chunks, and add to the garlic. Add capers to the bowl and process until all ingredients are minced, a few seconds

only. Put the canned tomatoes in a strainer and chop roughly with a paring knife, letting excess juice drain.

Heat the oil in a saucepan over moderate heat. Add the minced garlic, onion and capers and cook for about 5 minutes, until the mixture is soft. Stir in the drained chopped tomatoes, the white pepper and the basil. (Salt is probably not needed since clams are salty and so are capers.) Bring the mixture to a boil, stirring, then reduce heat to low, cover, and simmer for 30 minutes. Drain the clams, reserving the can liquid. Stir the clams and the parsley into the tomato sauce and keep over low heat, stirring, only long enough to

heat the clams. Adjust the texture of the sauce with a little of the drained clam juice, if necessary, and the salt and acid balance with lemon juice to taste.

Serve the sauce over 1 pound pasta, cooked and drained. Use it all when freshly made, for the clams become tough if reheated.

Pesto

(Basil and Garlic Sauce)

about 2 cups

2 ounces Parmesan cheese
2 to 4 garlic cloves
1½ cups fresh basil leaves, no stems
¼ cup pine nuts

½ teaspoon salt
¼ teaspoon freshly ground black pepper
½ cup olive oil

In a food processor fitted with the steel blade, process the cheese until evenly grated. Pour out the cheese on a sheet of wax paper. Reassemble the processor. Peel garlic cloves. Process basil leaves, pine nuts, garlic, salt and pepper to a green paste. Pour the olive oil through the tube, a little at a time, and process until the mixture is smooth. Scrape the purée into a mixing bowl and beat in the cheese.

Pesto can be refrigerated, tightly covered, for about a week. It can also be frozen and will keep for at least 6 weeks.

For easiest use, freeze pesto in ice-cube trays. Transfer the frozen blocks to a freezer bag. The small blocks can be defrosted quickly, and often that amount is all one needs for a recipe.

Spoon the desired amount over hot drained pasta and pour in about ¼ cup of the pasta cooking water. Toss to mix sauce and pasta well and serve at once. Pesto can also be added to soups and can enrich other sauces.

68

Fettuccine Alfredo

4 portions

1 pound fettuccine
2 tablespoons salt
1 tablespoon olive oil
4 tablespoons unsalted
    butter

4 ounces Parmesan cheese,
    grated (1 cup)
1 cup heavy cream
    freshly ground black
    pepper

Cook fettuccine in 6 quarts boiling water with 2 tablespoons salt and the tablespoon of oil until tender but firm, 5 to 7 minutes for dried pasta, 1 to 2 minutes for fresh pasta. Drain pasta and transfer to a warmed serving bowl. Cut the butter into small pieces and toss with the pasta. Add ½ cup of the cheese, the cream and a generous grinding of black pepper. Toss mixture well. Serve at once, accompanied with remaining cheese. Provide a pepper mill for more freshly ground spice.

Fettuccine alla Romana

4 portions

1 large onion
1 garlic clove
4 ounces mushrooms
5 tablespoons butter
2 cups canned peeled plum
    tomatoes
    salt

¼ teaspoon black pepper
¼ cup dry red wine
1 teaspoon sugar
1 pound fettuccine
2 tablespoons grated
    Parmesan cheese

Peel and chop the onion. Peel garlic and put through a press into the onion. Wipe mushrooms with a damp cloth, trim base of stems, and cut caps and stems into thin slices. Melt 4 tablespoons of the butter in a skillet over moderate heat. Add onion and garlic and cook for 5 to 7 minutes, until onion is soft and translucent but not brown. Add the tomatoes with the juices from the can, the sliced mushrooms, ½ teaspoon salt, the pepper, wine and sugar; stir well. Bring the liquid to a boil, cover the pan, reduce heat to low, and simmer for 20 minutes.

Meanwhile, bring 6 quarts water to a boil and add 2 tablespoons salt and the fettuccine. Boil for 5 to 7 minutes, until the pasta is firm but tender. Test it by removing and biting a strand. Drain fettuccine in a colander and transfer it to a warmed serving bowl. Stir remaining tablespoon of butter into the hot pasta and toss until melted. Pour the sauce over the pasta and sprinkle with grated cheese. Serve immediately.

Spaghetti alla Carbonara

(Spaghetti with Eggs and Bacon)

4 to 6 portions

4 ounces smoked bacon	⅓ cup chopped fresh parsley
1 garlic clove	2 tablespoons salt
1 tablespoon oil	1 pound spaghetti or spaghettini
3 large eggs	freshly ground black pepper
3 ounces Parmesan cheese, grated (¾ cup)	

Cut the bacon into small squares. Peel the garlic. Heat the oil in a skillet over moderate heat. Add the garlic and cook until it is brown; remove and discard it. Add bacon to the skillet and cook until crisp but not brown. With a slotted spoon lift bacon pieces to a plate. Break the eggs into a bowl and mix with a rotary egg beater or a whisk. Add cheese and parsley and mix lightly with a fork.

Bring 6 quarts water to a boil and add 2 tablespoons salt and the pasta. Cook spaghetti for 6 minutes, until tender but firm. If you are using spaghettini, cook for about 4 minutes. Keeping the pasta in the pot, pour out the cooking water. At once pour in the egg mixture and toss it with the pasta as quickly as possible, so the eggs cook on the hot pasta but do not become scrambled or fall into lumps. Add the bacon and freshly ground black pepper to taste and toss again. Serve immediately.

Variations: Instead of bacon, use 3 or 4 ounces prosciutto, chopped. Sauté 2 shallots or small onions, chopped, in the oil before adding the prosciutto. Do not use garlic in this. A few tablespoons of white wine can be added to the prosciutto, or a few tablespoons of cream can be added to the eggs.

Linguine with Butter and Cheese

4 to 6 portions

2 tablespoons salt	6 ounces butter
1 pound linguine	8 ounces Parmesan cheese

Bring 6 quarts water to a boil. Add the salt and the linguine and cook for 5 to 7 minutes, until pasta is firm but tender. Drain pasta and turn into a large deep serving bowl. Cut the butter into small cubes and drop into the pasta. Grate the cheese and add 1 cup of it to the pasta. Using 2 large spoons, toss everything together until butter and cheese have melted into the warm pasta and coated it. Serve immediately, with the remaining cup of cheese in a separate bowl.

Pasta Shells with Cream Cheese and Walnut Sauce

4 portions

Walnut Sauce (see Index)
3 to 5 tablespoons light cream

8 ounces cream cheese
1 tablespoon salt
12 ounces small pasta shells

Make the walnut sauce; at the end thin it with a few tablespoons extra light cream. Keep the sauce warm. Have the cream cheese cold; cut it into ½-inch cubes and place them on a plate. Cover with plastic wrap and return to refrigerator to keep cold.

Bring 4 quarts water to a boil. Add the salt and the pasta shells and cook for about 8 minutes, until shells are tender but firm. Drain and turn shells into a deep serving bowl. Pour the warm walnut sauce and also the cold cream cheese into the pasta and toss with 2 large spoons until well mixed. The hot pasta and sauce will start to melt the cheese but the center of the cheese cubes will remain unmelted. The contrast of the hot pasta and the cold cream cheese makes this dish unusual. Serve it as soon as it is well mixed.

Tagliatelle with Chicken-Liver and Wine Sauce

4 to 6 portions

8 ounces chicken livers
4 ounces mushrooms
2 tablespoons unsalted butter
1 tablespoon minced shallot
2 tablespoons flour
1 cup chicken stock

½ cup dry Marsala wine
salt
1 pound tagliatelle
¼ cup heavy cream
black pepper
2 tablespoons chopped fresh parsley

Wash and trim chicken livers and pat dry. Cut them into thin slices. Wipe mushrooms with a damp cloth, trim base of stems, and cut caps and stems into slices the same thickness as the slices of liver. Melt the butter in a saucepan. Add shallot and sauté for 1 minute. Add chicken livers and mushrooms and sauté for 4 minutes. Sprinkle in the flour and cook for 1 minute, stirring. Gradually stir in chicken stock and Marsala. Simmer gently for about 15 minutes.

Meanwhile, bring 6 quarts water to a boil. Add 2 tablespoons salt and the tagliatelle. Cook until pasta is firm but tender.

Add cream to chicken livers; simmer until the sauce is slightly reduced and thickened. Season to taste.

Drain cooked pasta, turn onto a warmed platter, and spoon chicken-liver sauce over the top. Sprinkle with chopped parsley.

Tagliatelle Verde with Tuna Sauce

4 to 6 portions

12 ounces canned water-packed tuna
¼ cup olive oil
2 tablespoons chopped fresh parsley
1¾ cups chicken stock, hot

1½ teaspoons black pepper
salt
1 pound tagliatelle verde (spinach-flavored green noodles)
1 tablespoon butter

Drain and flake the tuna. Heat the oil in a skillet over moderate heat. When oil is hot, reduce heat to low and add the tuna and 1½ tablespoons of the parsley. Cook, stirring, for 5 minutes. Add the stock and black pepper and cook for 5 minutes longer, stirring often.

Bring 6 quarts water to a boil and add 2 tablespoons salt and the spinach pasta. Cook until firm but tender, drain, and turn into a large serving bowl. Add the butter and toss the pasta with 2 large spoons until it is coated with butter. Pour the sauce over the pasta and sprinkle remaining parsley on top. Serve at once.

Tagliatelle Verde with Mushroom Sauce

4 portions

Mushroom Sauce

1	small onion
1	garlic clove
10	ounces small mushrooms
2	tablespoons butter
1	tablespoon olive oil
2	teaspoons chopped fresh parsley
1	tablespoon flour

6	tablespoons chicken stock
	salt and black pepper

12	ounces tagliatelle verde
1	tablespoon salt
1	tablespoon butter

First make the sauce: Peel and mince onion and garlic. Wipe mushrooms with a damp cloth, trim base of stems, and cut caps and stems into thin slices. Heat 2 tablespoons butter and the tablespoon of olive oil in a saucepan and cook the onion, garlic and parsley over low heat until soft. Sprinkle in the flour, then stir in the mushrooms, 4 tablespoons of the stock, and salt and pepper to taste. Simmer until the mushrooms are soft. There should be enough liquid to make a slightly thickened sauce, but if there is not enough, add remaining 2 tablespoons stock. Keep the sauce warm.

Bring 4 quarts water to a boil and add 1 tablespoon salt and the tagliatelle. Boil the pasta for about 8 minutes, until firm but tender, or until as tender as you like it. Drain the pasta and turn into a warmed serving bowl. Add the tablespoon of butter and toss to coat the strands with butter. Spoon the sauce on top and toss again. Serve as a first course.

Tagliatelle with Prosciutto

4 to 6 portions

4	small white onions	2	tablespoons salt
12	ounces prosciutto	1	pound tagliatelle
8	tablespoons unsalted butter	6	ounces Parmesan cheese, grated (1½ cups)
½	cup dry white wine	2	tablespoons chopped parsley
½	cup chicken stock		

Peel and mince the onions. Cut prosciutto into 2-inch strips. Melt the butter in a skillet over moderate heat. Add minced onions and cook, stirring, for 5 minutes. Add prosciutto strips and cook for 5 minutes longer. Pour in the wine and chicken stock and simmer over low heat until the liquid is reduced by half.

Bring 6 quarts water to a boil and add the salt and tagliatelle. Cook for about 8 minutes, until tender but firm. Drain and turn into a warmed serving bowl. Add the prosciutto mixture and toss with 2 large spoons until the pasta is coated with the sauce. Sprinkle ½ cup of the cheese on top, and serve the rest of the cheese separately. Sprinkle with chopped parsley.

Paglia e Fieno

(Straw and Hay Pasta with Veal and Mushrooms)

4 portions

1 small onion	salt and black pepper
6 slices of lean bacon	1 cup light cream
8 ounces fresh mushrooms	2 tablespoons chopped fresh parsley
5 tablespoons unsalted butter	6 ounces plain egg noodles
4 ounces boneless veal, ground (1 cup)	6 ounces green egg noodles
⅛ teaspoon crumbled dried orégano	2 ounces Parmesan cheese, grated (½ cup)

Peel and chop the onion. Chop the bacon strips. Wipe mushrooms with a damp cloth, trim base of stems, and slice caps and stems. Heat 4 tablespoons of the butter in a skillet over moderate heat. Add chopped onion and bacon and sauté, stirring occasionally, until onion is soft and translucent but not brown, 5 to 7 minutes. Add the ground veal and cook, stirring constantly, until the meat is well browned, about 5 minutes. Stir in mushrooms, orégano, and salt and black pepper to taste. Sauté until mushrooms are tender, about 5 minutes. Add cream and parsley to the skillet. Reduce heat to low and cook, stirring, for 3 to 5 minutes.

Bring 4 quarts water to a boil and add 1 tablespoon salt and the noodles. Boil noodles until firm and tender. Drain noodles and place in a warmed serving bowl; the green and white strands should be mingled. Add remaining tablespoon of butter and toss the pasta to coat it well. Pour veal and mushroom sauce over the noodles and again toss to mix. Serve immediately, with the grated cheese in a bowl.

Capellini alla Primavera

(Angel's-Hair Pasta with Vegetables)

4 portions

2 garlic cloves	2 cups very small cauliflowerets
2 carrots	1 tablespoon minced fresh basil
3 large tomatoes	⅛ teaspoon crumbled dried orégano
8 thin asparagus spears	salt and black pepper
12 mushrooms	1 pound capellini
20 snow peas	4 ounces Parmesan cheese, grated (1 cup)
1 small zucchini, 4 ounces	
8 tablespoons unsalted butter	
½ cup olive oil	
1 tablespoon minced shallot	

Peel garlic and put through a press. Scrape carrots and cut into thin slices. Peel and chop tomatoes. Wash asparagus, remove scales, and cut the tender portions into ½-inch diagonal slices. Wipe mushrooms with a damp cloth, trim base of stems, and cut caps and stems into thin slices. Wash snow peas; pull off stems and strings along both sides. Wash and trim zucchini and cut into thin slices.

Heat butter and oil in a large skillet over moderate heat. Sauté shallot and garlic for 1 minute. Add sliced carrots and cauliflowerets and sauté for 1 minute. Add chopped tomatoes, asparagus pieces, sliced mushrooms, snow peas and sliced zucchini. Keep stirring everything in the skillet as the vegetables are added. Sprinkle in the fresh and dried herbs and add salt and pepper to taste. Sauté and stir until vegetables are crisp-tender, 3 to 4 minutes.

Meanwhile, bring 6 quarts water to a boil. Add 2 tablespoons salt and the capellini and cook for about 3 minutes, until pasta is firm but tender; do not overcook this delicate pasta. Drain pasta and divide among 4 warmed dinner plates. Spoon vegetables over each portion and serve at once. Accompany with grated cheese.

74

Fettuccine with Herbs and Cheese

4 to 6 portions

1	pound fettuccine	½	teaspoon crumbled dried orégano
	salt	½	teaspoon black pepper
6	tablespoons butter	4	ounces Romano cheese, grated (1 cup)
3	garlic cloves		
3	tablespoons chopped fresh parsley		
1	tablespoon minced fresh basil, or 1½ teaspoons dried		

Bring 6 quarts water to a boil and add 2 tablespoons salt and the fettuccine noodles. Cook for about 7 minutes, until firm but tender. Drain and return to the pot.

Melt the butter in a saucepan over moderate heat. Peel the garlic cloves and put through a press into the butter. Add parsley, basil and orégano, and stir. Add the drained noodles to the saucepan and season with ½ teaspoon salt and the pepper. Using 2 large spoons, toss noodles in the butter until thoroughly coated. Stir in the grated cheese and mix in until the cheese is melted. Remove pan from heat, turn the pasta into a warmed serving bowl, and serve at once.

Ziti with Meatballs and Sauce

6 to 8 portions

1	tablespoon salt		**Tomato Sauce with Mushrooms and Peas**
1	tablespoon olive oil	1	large onion
1	pound ziti	2	garlic cloves
2	tablespoons butter	4	ounces mushrooms
	Meatballs	3	tablespoons olive oil
2	slices of white bread	1	cup shelled fresh peas
¼	cup milk	3½	cups canned peeled plum tomatoes
1½	pounds ground lean beef	¾	cup dry red wine
2	teaspoons grated lemon rind	⅓	cup tomato purée
⅔	cup dried bread crumbs	½	teaspoon salt
1	large egg	1	teaspoon black pepper
2	garlic cloves	1	teaspoon dried orégano
1	teaspoon salt	8	ounces Italian sausage
1	teaspoon black pepper	4	ounces mozzarella cheese, grated (1 cup)
1½	teaspoons dried orégano		
¼	cup olive oil		

First make the meatballs: Soak the slices of bread in the milk for 5 minutes. Break the bread into small chunks and drop into a mixing bowl. Add the ground beef, lemon rind, bread crumbs and egg. Peel garlic and put through a press into the mixture. Add salt, pepper and orégano. Beat mixture with a fork until well mixed. At the end you may need to mix by hand. Shape the mixture into walnut-size balls. Place meatballs on a large plate, cover, and chill them in the refrigerator for 30 minutes, or until you are ready to continue.

Make the sauce: Peel the onion and cut into thin slices. Peel garlic cloves and crush them. Wipe mushrooms with a damp cloth, trim base of stems, and slice caps and stems. Heat the oil in a large saucepan over moderate heat. Add onion and garlic and cook, stirring occasionally, for 5 to 7 minutes, until onion is soft and translucent but not brown. Add mushrooms and peas and cook for 3 minutes. Add the tomatoes with the juices from the can, the wine, tomato purée, salt, pepper and orégano; stir well to mix. Bring the liquid to a boil, reduce heat to low, cover, and simmer the sauce for 30 minutes. Remove sauce from heat.

Heat the oil for the meatballs in a large skillet over moderate heat. Add the meatballs, a few at a time, and fry, turning them on all sides, for 5 to 8 minutes, until evenly browned. Using a slotted spoon, transfer cooked meatballs to the pan of sauce. Brown remaining meatballs in the same way. Remove the casing from the sausage and cut it into 1-inch pieces. Brown the sausage in the skillet and transfer that to the sauce. Return saucepan to low heat and simmer for 30 minutes. Add the grated cheese to the sauce and stir until it is melted and well mixed.

Bring 6 quarts water to a boil and add the tablespoon of salt, the tablespoon of oil and the ziti. Cook ziti for 10 to 15 minutes, until tender but firm. Drain ziti in a colander, then turn into a large serving bowl. Add 2 tablespoons butter and toss with 2 spoons until the strands are well coated. Pour sauce and meatballs over the ziti; or pour a little sauce over the pasta and serve the rest with the meatballs in a separate bowl. Serve at once.

The meatballs and sauce can be used with many other kinds of pasta; spaghetti is good with this, and all sorts of macaroni. The pasta should be thicker rather than thinner, to combine well with the heavy sauce.

Rigatone with Sausage and Zucchini

6 portions

2 small onions
1 garlic clove
3 zucchini, about 1 pound altogether
1 red bell pepper
4 tablespoons unsalted butter
2 tablespoons olive oil
3½ cups canned peeled plum tomatoes
3 tablespoons tomato purée

salt
1 teaspoon black pepper
2 teaspoons minced fresh basil
1 pound hot Italian sausage
8 ounces sweet Italian sausage
1 pound rigatoni
4 ounces Parmesan cheese, grated (1 cup)

Peel and chop onions. Peel and crush garlic. Scrub and trim zucchini and cut them into thin slices. Wash red pepper, halve it, discard stem, seeds and ribs, and chop pepper. Melt 2 tablespoons of the butter with 1 tablespoon of the oil in a large saucepan over moderate heat. Add the onions, garlic, zucchini and red pepper and cook, stirring, for 5 to 7 minutes, until onions are soft and translucent but not brown. Add tomatoes with the juices from the can, the tomato purée, ½ teaspoon salt, the pepper and basil, and stir well to mix. Bring the liquid to a boil, reduce heat to low, and simmer the sauce for 15 minutes. Remove casings from the sausages and cut them into ½-inch slices. Stir sausage slices into the pan of sauce, cover, and simmer for 30 minutes longer.

Bring 6 quarts water to a boil and add 2 tablespoons salt and remaining tablespoon of oil. Add the rigatoni and cook for 12 to 15 minutes, until firm but tender. Remove pan from heat and drain the pasta in a colander. Turn pasta into a large serving bowl and add remaining 2 tablespoons butter and ¼ cup of the cheese. Using 2 large spoons, toss the mixture until all the strands are coated with butter and cheese.

Stir remaining cheese into the sauce and stir until cheese is melted. Pour the sauce over the pasta and serve at once.

Quadrettini with Spinach and Prosciutto

4 portions

8 ounces spinach
2 ounces prosciutto
6 tablespoons butter
salt
12 ounces quadrettini (flat pasta squares)
½ teaspoon black pepper

2 teaspoons minced fresh basil
½ teaspoon crumbled dried orégano
1 ounce Parmesan cheese, grated (¼ cup)
¼ cup chicken stock

Wash the spinach thoroughly. Cook in boiling water for 5 minutes, then drain, rinse in very cold water, and drain again, pressing to drain off as much water as possible. Chop the spinach. Chop the prosciutto. Melt the butter in a skillet over moderate heat. Add prosciutto and cook for 30 seconds. Add spinach and cook for 3 minutes, stirring to mix with prosciutto.

Bring 4 quarts water to a boil; add 1 tablespoon salt and the quadrettini. Boil the pasta for 6 to 8 minutes, until firm but tender. Drain well. Add quadrettini to the skillet and mix in 1 teaspoon salt, the pepper, basil, orégano, grated cheese and chicken stock. Bring to a boil, stirring occasionally. Reduce heat to low and simmer for 5 minutes. Remove pan from heat and turn the mixture into a warmed serving dish. Serve immediately.

Perciatelli with Green Pea Sauce

4 portions

1	medium-size onion			salt
4	slices of bacon		½	teaspoon black pepper
3	pounds fresh green peas in pods		½	cup light cream
2	tablespoons olive oil		12	ounces perciatelli
1	teaspoon minced fresh basil, or ½ teaspoon dried		2	tablespoons butter
2	teaspoons snipped fresh dill, or 1 teaspoon dried		2	ounces Parmesan cheese, grated (½ cup)

Peel and chop the onion. Cut bacon into small pieces. Shell the peas; there should be 3 cups. Heat the oil in a saucepan over moderate heat. When hot, add onion and bacon and cook, stirring constantly, for 5 to 7 minutes, until bacon is crisp. Add basil, dill, 1 teaspoon salt, the pepper and the shelled peas. Pour in 1 cup water and bring to a boil. Reduce heat to low and simmer the mixture for 10 to 12 minutes, until peas are tender. (If they are not done, cook them a little longer.) Remove pan from heat and purée the contents through a food mill or in an electric blender.

Return the puréed sauce to the pan and stir in the cream. Set the pan over low heat and simmer the sauce, stirring occasionally, for 2 minutes, until hot. Taste the sauce and add more salt and pepper if needed. Pour sauce into a warmed serving bowl and keep warm.

Bring 4 quarts water to a boil and add 1 tablespoon salt and the perciatelli. Cook for 8 to 10 minutes, until firm but tender. Drain and return to the pot. Add the butter to the pasta and toss until the strands are all coated with butter. Pour the buttered perciatelli into a warmed serving bowl. Accompany with the sauce in its bowl and the grated cheese.

78

Fusilli with Tomatoes and Cheese

4 portions

1	medium-size onion	2	tablespoons tomato purée
4	ounces Bel Paese cheese	1	teaspoon crumbled dried
2	ounces Parmesan cheese		orégano
	grated (½ cup)		salt
2	tablespoons vegetable oil	½	teaspoon black pepper
2	cups canned peeled plum	1	pound fusilli
	tomatoes		

Peel and chop the onion. Cut Bel Paese cheese into small cubes and grate the Parmesan cheese. Heat the oil in a skillet over moderate heat. When hot, add the onion and cook, stirring occasionally, for 5 to 7 minutes, until soft and translucent but not brown. Add the tomatoes, the juice from the can, the tomato purée, orégano, ½ teaspoon salt and the black pepper; stir well. Bring to a boil over high heat, reduce heat to low, cover the pan, and simmer for 20 minutes, stirring occasionally.

Bring 6 quarts water to a boil and add 2 tablespoons salt and the fusilli. Cook for 8 to 10 minutes, until pasta is firm but tender. Drain fusilli in a colander and return them to the saucepan. Add tomato sauce and both cheeses to the pasta. Set the pan over low heat and toss the fusilli with 2 forks until the cheeses have melted. Turn fusilli and sauce into a warmed serving bowl and serve at once.

Farfalle with Zucchini and Pimiento

6 portions

3	shallots	1	pound farfalle
2	pounds small zucchini	4	ounces grated pizza cheese
2	pimientos		(a mixture of mozzarella
4	to 6 tablespoons olive oil		and Parmesan)
1	tablespoon lemon juice		
	salt		

Peel and mince the shallots. Wash and trim zucchini and cut into ½-inch cubes. Rinse pimientos to get rid of all the seeds and the canning juices, and cut pimientos into thin strips. Heat 3 tablespoons of the oil in a large skillet over moderate heat and sauté shallots until soft; do not let them brown. Add zucchini to the pan and sauté, stirring, until they are crisp-tender; do not let them become mushy. If the pan becomes dry add up to 2 tablespoons more oil. Stir in pimiento strips and lemon juice and cook for 1 minute longer. Remove pan from heat and stir in ½ teaspoon salt, or to taste.

Bring 6 quarts water to a boil and add 2 tablespoons salt, 1 tablespoon oil and the farfalle. Cook for about 6 minutes, or until pasta is done to your taste. Drain pasta in a colander and return to the pot. Pour in the zucchini mixture, toss with 2 spoons, sprinkle the cheese on top, and serve at once.

Cavatelli with Almonds and Cream

4 portions

8	ounces shelled almonds	2	tablespoons chopped fresh
	sea salt		parsley
3	tablespoons olive oil	4	ounces Parmesan cheese,
1	pound cavatelli		grated (1 cup)
1	garlic clove	1	teaspoon black pepper
		1	cup light cream

Preheat oven to 375°F. Put the almonds in a heatproof bowl and pour in enough boiling water to cover them. Let them soak for 10 minutes, then pour off the water. Peel the almonds: Pinch the skin at the rounder end, and the nut will pop out. Continue until all are peeled; if they become hard to work with, cover them with hot water again, then drain. Put the peeled almonds in a shallow heatproof dish and slide into the preheated oven. Bake for 25 minutes, until almonds are golden brown. Remove dish from the oven and sprinkle 1 teaspoon sea salt over the nuts.

Bring 6 quarts water to a boil. Add 2 tablespoons sea salt and 1 tablespoon olive oil and drop in the cavatelli. Cook for 12 to 15 minutes, until pasta is firm but tender; or cook until it is as soft as you like. If the cavatelli are frozen, allow an extra 2 minutes of cooking time. Drain the pasta in a colander and return to the pan.

Peel the garlic and put through a press into the pasta. Add the parsley, grated cheese, black pepper and cream. Using 2 large spoons, toss the ingredients together until well combined. Add the toasted almonds and toss again until almonds are mixed in. Transfer to a heated serving bowl and serve immediately.

Vermicelli with Green Sauce

4 to 6 portions

1	bunch of fresh flat-leaf parsley	2	teaspoons black pepper
8	garlic cloves	2	tablespoons salt
½	cup olive oil	1	pound vermicelli

Wash and dry the parsley. Cut all the leaves from the stems and drop into the bowl of a food processor fitted with the steel blade. Chop until you have 10 tablespoons parsley. (If you have chopped much more than that, freeze it in ice-cube trays and store for future sauces.) Peel garlic cloves and put through a press. Heat the oil in a saucepan over moderate heat. When hot, add garlic and cook, stirring, for 3 minutes, until the puréed garlic begins to turn golden. Add parsley and black pepper and simmer the sauce, still stirring, for 5 minutes longer. Remove pan from heat but keep the sauce warm.

Bring 6 quarts water to a boil and add the salt and the vermicelli. Boil the pasta for about 3 minutes, until firm but tender; do not overcook vermicelli, as it can quickly become mushy. Drain pasta and turn into a large deep serving bowl. Pour the green sauce into the pasta and toss with 2 spoons until pasta is thoroughly coated. Serve the green-flecked pasta at once.

Part Four
PÂTE À CHOUX

Antonin Carême, the great nineteenth-century chef who overcame poverty and illiteracy to become "the cook of kings and king of cooks," presided in the kitchens of, among other notables, Talleyrand, Czar Alexander I of Russia, England's Prince Regent (the future King George IV) and Baron de Rothschild, who was happy to pay Carême a salary that far exceeded that of any of his former employees. Carême is largely credited with restoring grandeur and glory to French cuisine after the ravages and convulsions of the Revolution.

Among the most notable of his many accomplishments was the innovation and artistry that he brought to the art of *pâtisserie* (pastry making). "There are five branches of art:" wrote Carême, "painting, sculpture, poetry, music and architecture, the main branch of which is pastry making."

Carême was magisterial, pedantic, even pompous, but he practiced what he preached. Through discipline and force of will he taught himself to read and to draw and spent hours every day for ten years studying architecture in the Print Room of the Bibliothèque Royale in Paris. He began by copying, "then drawing, then carrying out in pastry, monumental pieces such as an octagonal Indian pavilion with orange roofs and a tri-tiered base, fluted sides and innumerable ornaments, or a scene of a waterfall, fountain, and broken Grecian arches and columns in the neoclassic tradition of Romantic landscape painters" (Barbara Norman, *Tales of the Table*).

No one today has the patience, skill or desire to recreate these magnificent pastry edifices, but Carême's legacy lives on in the various pastry-making techniques he developed and codified. Among the most versatile of these is the *pâte à choux* which is used in creating a great many desserts as well as savory dishes. Cream puffs, éclairs, profiteroles, beignets soufflés, the gâteau Saint-Honoré, croquembouche and Paris-Brest are some of the many elegant desserts that can be made with *pâte à choux*.

Strictly speaking, *pâte à choux* is not a pastry at all but a *panade*—a combination of water, butter and flour—into which eggs are beaten until they are fully incorporated. The technique of making *pâte à choux* is simplicity itself, although without the help of a food processor beating the eggs into the panade can be quite strenuous.

Madeleine Kamman writes that if you "Ask any French cook or chef what he first made in the kitchen where he apprenticed, the answer is sure to be '... *de la pâte à choux*...' or cream-puff paste. It is common in a French restaurant kitchen to see a young fellow standing on a box in front of a blazing stove and laboriously stirring cream-puff paste. Let the poor child ask the chef whether the paste is dry enough and the *gros bonnet* (the big hat of the main chef) will answer crossly: 'Are you kidding? Do you call this a dry paste? Go on, fellow, at least five more minutes!' The poor *marmiton* (apprentice cook) is disgusted, but the *gros bonnet* knows what he is talking about" *(The Making of a Cook).*

The point is that while you are stirring or beating the paste in a pot over medium heat, you are extracting and evaporating as much water as possible from the paste, and the more water you extract, the more eggs the paste will be able to absorb and the lighter, airier and puffier your baked pastry will be.

Pâte à choux, or cream-puff paste, is a totally different product from flaky pastry. This dough, moist with eggs, is actually a thick batter. It couldn't be easier to make: water (and sometimes milk) and butter are boiled together, flour is added and the resulting thick paste cooked briefly, then eggs are beaten in. That's it. The mixture is spooned or piped from a pastry bag into individual or large shapes, and baked until golden. During its time in the oven, the dough puffs up dramatically, forming the weightless, air-filled structures we know as cream puffs, éclairs, and other similar pastries.

Sweet pastries are the best-known items made with *pâte à choux.* The name of this dough, by the way, means "cabbage paste," which is derived from the shape of cream puffs, said to resemble small heads of cabbage. When piped in miniature size, the puffs are called *profiteroles.* These are filled with whipped cream, liqueur-scented pastry cream, or ice cream, and often served with a hot chocolate sauce. Eclairs are usually filled with a coffee- or chocolate-flavored custard, and are sometimes baked in tiny versions called *carolines.* Some bakers also fashion small cream-filled swans from *pâte à choux.*

Larger sweet pastries made with this dough include the *Paris-Brest,* a buttercream-filled ring, and two spectacular cakes for special occasions. *Gâteau Saint-Honoré* is named after the patron saint of pastry cooks, and consists of a layer of pastry topped with a halo of caramel-glazed cream puffs, the entire construction filled with a rich custard lightened with egg whites. A *croquembouche* (literally, "crunches in the mouth") is a pyramid-shaped tower of cream-filled puffs, held together with caramel.

These sweet pastries hardly exhaust the uses for *pâte à choux.* This is where its real versatility begins. In Burgundy, the dough is mixed with cubes of cheese and baked in a large ring called a *gougère;* this is enjoyed as a snack with the superb local red wines. Smaller individual *gougères* can be made in the same way. An interesting supper dish consists of a *gougère* which is split, *Paris-Brest*-fashion, and filled with a savory sauced mixture. Small puffs can be split open and filled with any of dozens of cream, cheese, vegetable, fish, or meat fillings to make light hors d'oeuvres. The tiniest *choux,* called *mandeln* ("little nuts") in Jewish cooking, are sprinkled into soups.

Pâte à choux also serves as a binder for several mixtures which need the added strength provided by its egg and flour content. These include gnocchi, *dauphine* potatoes (breaded fried potato puffs), some fish pâtés, and the classic fish dumplings of Lyon, called *quenelles.* Without the *pâte à choux* binder, these fish items can emerge watery after baking or poaching.

Even more interesting is that this same dough can be deep-fried in small spoonfuls, to form *beignets soufflés,* or light fritters. These are a beguiling dessert, often studded with fresh fruit and served with an apricot sauce. When the batter is combined with savory ingredients such as cheese, ham, or seafood, *beignets* are excellent appetizer snacks, but they must be prepared at the last moment if they are to be light and crisp.

The crucial thing to remember with *pâte à choux* is not to be intimidated and to work with swift motions.

PÂTE À CHOUX

The results are so impressive it is hard to believe that the making of cream-puff paste is really simple. It requires only a minimum of equipment and time and a good strong arm for beating. A food processor makes the process even easier. Once made, the paste can be formed into puffs with 2 tablespoons or teaspoons; it is much easier and faster, however, to use a pastry bag. For forming éclairs, a pastry bag is essential.

There are certain basic rules you should stick to when making chou paste.

Don't attempt to double the basic recipe. It is better to make 2 batches. If the yield is more than you require, refrigerate the leftover dough for other uses.

Have all your ingredients at room temperature and measured before you start.

Avoid making chou paste on a very damp or humid day.

Once you start you must work rapidly and without interruption.

The chou paste should be warm when it is formed for baking. If you must make it ahead of time, brush the top with melted butter to prevent formation of a crust on the dough, cover tightly, and refrigerate. Allow 2 hours at room temperature, after it is removed from the refrigerator, before forming for baking. Freezing the chou paste is not recommended, as the dough will not rise as much as it should after it has been frozen.

Baked unfilled puffs can be stored in an airtight container for up to 3 days. To insure their crispness, heat them in a preheated 350°F oven for 2 to 3 minutes before adding the filling. Baked unfilled puffs can be frozen if wrapped tightly in plastic wrap and foil. Before using, bake them without defrosting in a preheated 325°F oven for 5 to 6 minutes, or just until they are crisp.

Baked puffs should be cooled before being filled. This is particularly important if the filling is a pastry cream. If the shells are hot, it can cause the pastry cream to curdle.

For best results the puffs should be served as soon as possible after being filled. There is an exception to this rule: If the filling is ice cream, fill the shells with slightly softened ice cream and then freeze them. When frozen, wrap them tightly in plastic wrap and foil and store in your freezer for a great dessert in an emergency or when you are pressed for time. They will keep for several weeks.

Basic Ingredients

Flour. The flour can be all-purpose flour or unbleached flour (bread flour). Some chefs feel that the higher gluten content of the bread flour gives a better puff or rise.

Shortening. Either unsalted butter or margarine can be used, but the butter will give a much better flavor.

Pâte à Choux (Cream-Puff Dough)

makes enough for 12 to 18 medium-size cream puffs or éclairs, or 48 profiteroles, or 1 small pastry ring

8 tablespoons unsalted butter, softened
½ teaspoon salt
1 cup water
1 cup sifted all-purpose flour
4 large eggs, at room temperature

Small Batch Pâte à Choux

makes 6 to 10 medium-size éclairs or cream puffs, or 24 profiteroles

4 tablespoons unsalted butter
  pinch of salt
½ cup water
1 teaspoon sugar
½ cup sifted all-purpose flour
2 large eggs

1 Place softened butter, salt and water in a deep, flat-bottomed saucepan over moderate heat. Bring slowly to a boil, stirring.

5 Using a wooden spoon, beat the egg until it is incorporated in the mixture.

Eggs. Eggs are the leavening agent in the paste which produces the expansion that creates the puff. Large eggs should be used.

Liquid. Water provides steam to raise the puff and also hydrates the protein and starch in the flour. Some chefs use ¼ cup milk and ¾ cup water, rather than the more usual 1 cup water.

Salt. A small amount of salt, usually ¼ teaspoon, is added purely to enhance the flavor and contribute to the baking process.

Sugar. A small quantity of sugar, usually 1 teaspoon, is added when the chou paste is for a dessert. Occasionally the amount of sugar is increased to 1 tablespoon, as in the making of *beignets.*

Equipment

In addition to the usual measuring cups and measuring spoons, you will need a heavy-bottomed saucepan, 1½- or 2-quart size, and a wooden spatula or spoon. A pastry bag with different-size tips is an invaluable tool and speeds up the process of forming the puffs. A pastry brush or goose feather brush is used to paint the tops of the puffs with egg wash. You will also need 2 baking sheets. Be sure that the sheets are the right size for your oven, at least 1 inch smaller on all 4 sides than your oven shelf. This allows for proper air circulation or convection. Lining the baking sheets with foil or parchment is also a big help. If by any chance the egg wash drips, it is a nuisance to get off an unlined baking sheet after it has cooked on.

A food processor, hand-held electric beater or an electric mixer with a pastry paddle will make the whole process effortless and quick.

2 Remove pan from the heat and add the flour all at once. Beat with a wooden spoon until smooth.

3 Return pan to very low heat and beat vigorously for 1 to 2 minutes until the mixture forms a smooth ball.

4 Remove pan from heat; allow to cool for 2 minutes. Drop in 1 egg.

6 Continue adding the eggs, one at a time, beating vigorously after each addition.

7 Continue beating until consistency is smooth. The dough should be stiff without being heavy.

8 Spoon or pipe the dough onto prepared baking sheet in accordance with recipe use.

Basic Technique

Have your ingredients at room temperature. Sift the flour before measuring it, and set it aside on a piece of wax paper. The butter should be slightly softened. If it is hard, cut it into pieces so it will melt rapidly.

Following the basic recipe, place the water, butter, salt and sugar in a saucepan and bring the mixture to a full rolling boil. Stop the cooking after the butter is completely melted and the entire surface of the liquid is boiling. You do not want to evaporate the water. Remove the pan from the heat and add the flour all at once. Beat hard with a wooden spoon until the mixture is completely smooth. When it is completely blended, return the pan to the stove over moderate heat for 1 to 2 minutes, beating vigorously the whole time. The mixture will form a mass and leave the sides of the pan. When you see a light film on the bottom of the pan, immediately remove the pan from the heat. The film indicates that you have evaporated the necessary amount of water from the mixture.

At this stage the mixture is too hot for the addition of the eggs as they would start to cook rather than blending in. Allow 2 to 3 minutes for the mixture to cool. Make a well in the middle of the paste with the wooden spoon. Break an egg into the well and beat until it is completely absorbed. Continue to add the eggs, one at a time, beating well after each addition. The third and fourth eggs will be absorbed more slowly. Continue to beat for a few moments to be sure that the mixture is smooth and completely blended. It will be very shiny in appearance, stiff enough to form a soft peak when lifted with a spoon.

The chou paste is now ready to be formed into specific shapes.

Electric Mixer Technique. Scald the bowl of your mixer with hot water. Drain it and dry it. This warming of the bowl will allow the cooked paste to remain warm.

Cook the water and butter as outlined in the basic technique. Add the flour and continue beating by hand.

Transfer the mixture to the warm bowl of the beater. Add the eggs, one at a time, beating at low speed to prevent splattering, then at high speed to incorporate them thoroughly. Alternatively, put the 4 eggs into a small bowl and beat them very lightly and briefly. The lightly beaten eggs are added, ¼ cup at a time. After all the eggs have been absorbed, beat the mixture for 2 to 3 seconds more. The paste is now ready for forming.

Hand-Held Electric Beater Technique. Follow the directions for cooking the basic water, butter and flour mixture. When the mixture has cooled enough to add the eggs, start with the first egg, at low speed to prevent spattering. Raise the speed when the egg is absorbed to blend it thoroughly. Lower the speed before adding the second egg, then raise it after the egg is absorbed. Continue in this manner until all the eggs are added and the mixture is smooth, stiff and shiny.

Food Processor Technique I. Follow the directions for cooking the basic water, butter and flour mixture. When it has cooled slightly, transfer it to the work bowl of the food processor fitted with the steel blade. With the motor running, add the eggs one at a time, allowing each to be absorbed before the next one is added. About 10 seconds of blending time should be sufficient for each egg to be incorporated. After the last egg has been blended, remove the cover, scrape down the sides of the work bowl, and process for about 20 seconds.

Food Processor Technique II. Place the flour in the work bowl of the processor fitted with the steel blade. In a heavy pan bring the water, butter and salt to a full rolling boil. With the motor running, pour the boiling hot mixture into the feed tube, slowly and steadily. After all the liquid has been added, process the mixture for about 45 seconds. The paste should be thick and shiny. Add the eggs one at a time. With the motor running, add the first egg through the feed tube and process for 10 seconds. Continue with the remaining eggs, processing for 10 seconds each time. After the last egg has been

1 Lightly brush baking sheet with melted fat. Sift flour over the surface. Preheat oven to 425°F. Make pastry. Allow to cool slightly.

5 For puffs, use a plain tube or fancy nozzle; fill piping bag. Hold bag vertically; press out required amount for small or large shapes.

7 Bake at the middle level of oven. Reduce oven temperature to 375°F and cook until well puffed and browned.

2 Using spoon handle, draw guidelines on prepared sheet. For ring shapes, mark around plate or pastry cutter of the required size.

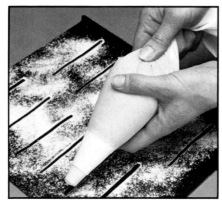

3 For éclairs, fill a piping bag fitted with a #9 plain round tube. Hold at a 45-degree angle just above marked sheet; press bag.

4 Pipe pastry across sheet following marked lines. At line end, raise nozzle; use a wet round-bladed knife to cut off the pastry.

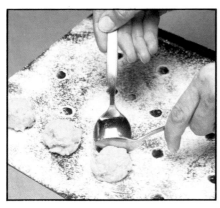

OR Use a teaspoon or tablespoon to drop pastry onto sheet, using pastry straight from pan. Scrape spoon clean with a second spoon.

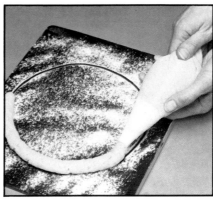

6 To make rings, mark ring on baking sheet. Fit piping bag with plain or fancy nozzle. Hold at 45-degree angle; pipe in a circle.

OR Pipe plain or fancy ball shapes so that they touch each other to form a crown, following a circle you have marked on the sheet.

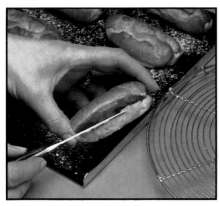

8 Remove from oven. Using a sharp knife, slit the side of each pastry to allow steam to escape.

9 Transfer pastry to wire rack. When cool, fill with desired sweet or savory filling.

10 To ice éclairs, make a glacé icing, flavoring it as wished. Dip top of filled éclair in the icing. Leave on wire rack to set icing.

88

added, remove the cover, scrape down the sides of the work bowl, and process for 20 seconds. The mixture is now ready to be formed and baked.

Forming Chou Pastry

Because chou paste is a stiff mixture which holds its shape, it is easy to form into different shapes, such as small puffs, large puffs, éclairs and rings. The pastry expands to 2 or 3 times its size during the baking process, so ample space must be left between the puffs on the baking sheets.

A pastry bag is by far the fastest and neatest way to form any of the shapes. Small and large puffs can be shaped with 2 spoons, teaspoons for small puffs and tablespoons for large ones. Drop a heaping spoonful onto the prepared sheet and use the second spoon, which has been dipped into cold water, to scrape the mixture off the first spoon. Place the shapes as you form them on a baking sheet lined with foil or parchment paper; if you prefer, use a baking sheet that has been lightly greased and then floured, with the excess flour knocked off.

If you are forming the paste into éclairs or a ring, it is preferable to grease and flour the baking sheet, knocking off the excess flour. Trace the outlines of the éclair shapes lightly with the tip of a spoon, or a chopstick, as a guide for shaping uniform sizes.

If you are forming a ring, invert a cake pan so that the rim makes a circular mark on the lightly floured surface. You now have an outline to follow when piping out the paste.

Puffs for frying, such as *beignets,* are piped or spooned directly into the hot fat in which they are to be fried.

Beignets are deep-fried morsels of chou paste. The dough is prepared in the standard way. Oil (corn oil has the least taste) is heated in a pan to 360°F and spoonfuls of dough are dropped into the hot oil for about 5 minutes until crisp and golden. They are drained on paper towels, sprinkled with powdered sugar, and served with jam, strawberry preserves, raspberry preserves (strained and heated), apricot sauce or honey.

Profiteroles are tiny puffs formed from a teaspoon of dough. With a second spoon dipped into cold water, push the spoonful of dough onto a lined (or buttered and floured) baking sheet. Allow a generous inch between the mounds. With a pastry bag use a #3 or #4 plain round tube, ¼ inch or less.

For large *cream puffs,* use a heaping tablespoon of dough and a second spoon to push the dough onto the baking sheet. With a pastry bag use a #9 plain round tube (about ¾ inch).

For *éclairs,* use a pastry bag with the #9 plain round tube. The dough should be piped out about 5 inches long and 1 inch wide.

For pastry rings, such as are used in *Paris-Brest* or *Gâteau Saint-Honoré,* the #9 tube is also used.

Glazing the Pastry Shells

Prepare an egg wash (or *dorure*): Beat 1 egg with 1 teaspoon water in a small bowl. Or beat the egg with 1 tablespoon milk. With a pastry brush, goose-feather brush or the tip of a finger, lightly brush the tops of the formed puffs with the egg wash. Smooth down any points or peaks to give a smooth professional look. Be careful not to let the egg wash drip down the sides as this can interfere with the rising.

Baking the Pastry

The pastry requires a very hot, preheated oven in order to puff up as it should. If you are baking 2 sheets of puffs, adjust the oven racks, one at the upper third level and the other at the lower third level. If only one baking sheet is being used, adjust the rack to the middle level.

Preheat oven to 425°F for at least 10 minutes. Place the puffs in the oven and bake for 15 minutes. You must not open the oven door at any time during the baking. After 15 minutes, lower the oven temperature to 375°F and con-

makes 1½ cups

2 tablespoons flour
1 cup milk
⅛ teaspoon salt
5 tablespoons sugar
4 large egg yolks
1 egg white
1 teaspoon vanilla extract

• Chocolate flavor: Fold 2 ounces (2 squares) melted unsweetened chocolate into the hot cream.
• Coffee flavor: Add 1 tablespoon extra-strong prepared coffee to the cooked cream.
• Fruit flavors: When completely cold, fold in an equal amount of puréed fruit.

4 Set the bowl over a pan of very hot water over low heat. Stir continuously until mixture thickens to a smooth custard.

tinue baking éclairs or large puffs for about 10 minutes, tiny puffs for about 5 minutes. Larger rings may take 40 to 50 minutes in all, depending on the recipe.

The shells will be crisp when done. Tap them gently to judge their crispness. They should sound hollow and look golden brown. When the puffs are done, remove one sheet from the oven and quickly pierce each puff with a skewer or the tip of a sharp knife to release any steam which might still be trapped inside. When all the puffs have been pierced, return the sheets to the turned-off oven and leave them for 10 to 15 minutes with the oven door

Crème Pâtissière (Pastry Cream)

1 Sift flour into bowl. Add 4 table-spoons of the milk and stir until smooth. Add the rest of the milk, gradually, then the salt and sugar, and transfer to a heavy-bottomed saucepan over medium heat

2 Place the yolks in a small bowl and beat until creamy.

3 When milk and flour mixture is thick and smooth, stir a little of the hot sauce into the egg yolks, then add the egg yolks to the saucepan, stirring briskly. Cook for just a second or two. Scrape the mixture into a bowl.

5 Remove bowl from heat. In a small bowl, beat the egg white until stiff.

6 Fold the egg white into the warm pastry cream and stir lightly for about 2 minutes, again over the hot water.

7 To flavor, stir the vanilla extract, melted chocolate or hot coffee into the warm cream. Fruit can be added only when the pastry cream is completely cold.

ajar. This helps to dry out the interiors thoroughly. If by any chance some of the puffs or éclairs are not completely dried out inside, remove any soft dough with the tip of a spoon.

Transfer the puffs to a wire rack to cool completely before filling with pastry cream, whipped cream or other filling.

Fillings for Cream Puffs and Eclairs

With the exception of an ice-cream filling, which can be done ahead of time and frozen, it is best to fill the baked and cooled shells as close to serving time as possible so as to preserve their crispness.

Puffs and éclairs may be filled in two ways: The baked pastry can be split into halves and the filling can be spooned or piped into the lower half and the top replaced. Or it can be filled by piercing a hole in the bottom and piping in the filling.

There are many fillings used for puffs and éclairs: vanilla custard, cooked and chilled; sweetened and flavored whipped cream; chocolate pastry cream; coffee-flavored pastry cream; lemon filling; puréed fruit mixed with whipped cream; buttercreams; chestnut cream, etc.

Toppings and Icings for Puffs and Eclairs

Cream puffs are often topped with powdered sugar after filling, but many times an icing is dribbled over the top. Small puffs for *profiteroles* are traditionally served with a hot chocolate sauce, and éclairs are always topped with a thin icing.

To make a professional-looking shiny icing you will need to have on hand plain simple syrup. Simple syrup is easily made; it can be kept in a covered jar, at room temperature, almost indefinitely to use as a sweetener with meringues, buttercreams, sauces, etc.

FILLINGS

Flavored Whipped Cream

makes 2 cups

1   cup heavy cream
1   to 2 tablespoons superfine
     sugar

1   teaspoon vanilla extract

Chill the mixing bowl or place it over ice. Beat the cream with an egg beater or electric mixer until it starts to thicken. Beat in the sugar and vanilla and beat until stiff. If not used at once, refrigerate. Try to use cream within 2 or 3 hours.

The following flavorings can be added to each cup of whipped cream: (fold the flavorings in after the cream is whipped) 2 tablespoons sifted dark unsweetened cocoa powder; 2 to 4 tablespoons rum, Cognac or any liqueur; ½ cup Praline (recipe follows); 1 teaspoon instant coffee powder.

Increasing the Yield of Whipped Cream. Add 1 egg white for each cup of cream. Beat the egg white until it holds soft peaks. Stir in 1 ½ tablespoons superfine sugar. Beat until very stiff. Fold into the whipped and flavored cream.

Praline

makes 1¾ cups

1 cup granulated sugar
1 tablespoon lemon juice

¾ cup blanched almonds, toasted and chopped medium fine, or ¾ cup mixed toasted chopped almonds and toasted chopped hazelnuts

Combine sugar and lemon juice in a heavy pan. Melt over low heat, stirring constantly with a wooden spoon. When mixture is a deep golden color and the sugar is dissolved, add the nuts, stirring. Pour the mixture out on a well-oiled surface, a marble slab or large flat pan or baking sheet. When completely cool, break the mixture into pieces and grind the pieces in a blender or food processor to a powder. Store the powder in an airtight jar.

Almond Cream Filling

makes 2½ cups

4 tablespoons unsalted butter
1 cup almond paste
1 cup milk or light cream
½ cup sugar

½ cup toasted almonds, ground
6 egg yolks, beaten
1 teaspoon vanilla extract
¼ teaspoon almond extract

Cream the butter until soft. Add the almond paste, a little at a time, alternating with the milk. Stir in the sugar and finally the ground almonds. Transfer to a saucepan. Over medium heat, cook the mixture until it becomes thick. Stir a few tablespoons of the hot cream into the beaten egg yolks, then add the egg yolks to the hot cream, stirring briskly.

Return the pan to low heat and continue to cook. Stir constantly until the cream thickens a little more. Be careful not to let it boil. Remove from heat and beat to cool it slightly. When the mixture has cooled, add the vanilla and almond extracts.

Chestnut Cream Filling

enough for 12 éclairs or puffs

12 ounces sweetened chestnuts or chestnut pieces in syrup
6 ounces unsalted butter

2 teaspoons rum, preferably light
1 cup heavy cream, whipped

In a food processor or blender combine the chestnuts, butter and rum and blend until smooth. If the butter should separate, transfer the mixture to a saucepan over low heat. Stir until the mixture is smooth and refrigerate until cool.

Whip the cream until stiff. Fold one third of the chestnut mixture into the cream. Add the rest of the chestnut mixture, folding it in gently just until blended.

TOPPINGS AND ICINGS

Simple Syrup

makes about 2 cups

2½ cups sugar
¾ cup white corn syrup

1¼ cups water

Combine sugar, corn syrup and water in a large saucepan. Stir over low heat until sugar is dissolved. When the mixture is completely clear-looking, wash down the sides of the pan with a brush dipped into cold water. Place cover on pan and cook over low heat for 5 minutes. The resulting steam will further dissolve any sugar crystals. Remove lid, raise the heat, and boil for 5 minutes without stirring.

When the syrup has cooled, pour it into a jar and cover tightly. With simple syrup you will be able to make a "mock fondant." This is much easier to make than a true fondant, and the resulting shiny icing gives a professional appearance to puffs and éclairs.

Mock Fondant

enough for about 18 éclairs or cream puffs

½ cup cooled Simple Syrup (preceding recipe)
1½ cups sifted confectioners' sugar

1 teaspoon egg white
1 teaspoon melted butter

Pour the syrup into a heavy-bottomed saucepan and add the sugar. You will have a stiff paste. Place the pan over low heat and cook, stirring constantly, until the mixture is lukewarm. Avoid overheating or the icing will not be shiny. Beat in the egg white and melted butter. If the icing is too thick, add a bit more syrup. If too thin, add more sugar.

Flavor with any of the following: 1 ounce (1 square) unsweetened chocolate, melted; 1 tablespoon prepared extra-strong coffee; 2 tablespoons rum or any liqueur; 1 teaspoon vanilla extract.

The resulting fondant should be thick enough to cover the éclair but soft enough to pour and spread by itself.

Mocha Frosting

enough for 6 éclairs or puffs

2 tablespoons butter
1 teaspoon powdered instant coffee

½ cup confectioners' sugar
1 tablespoon heavy cream

Melt the butter in a small heavy-bottomed pan and stir in the coffee and confectioners' sugar. Stir briskly with a whisk. Add the cream, beating to blend it in. Let the frosting cool and thicken before using.

Chocolate Frosting

enough for 6 éclairs or puffs

2 tablespoons butter
1½ ounces (1½ squares) semisweet chocolate

2 tablespoons milk
½ cup confectioners' sugar

Place butter and chocolate in a heavy-bottomed pan. Heat and stir until the chocolate is melted. Remove pan from heat and add the milk gradually, stirring to blend it well. Add the sugar and stir briskly to blend frosting completely.

Caramel Glaze

enough for about 12 eclairs or puffs

2 cups granulated sugar
¼ teaspoon cream of tartar

¾ cup water

Place sugar, cream of tartar and water in a heavy-bottomed pan over moderate heat. Stir until the sugar dissolves. Stop stirring. Allow the syrup to cook until it develops a medium caramel color, golden brown. Set the pan in a pan of cold water to stop further cooking.

If the glaze should set before you have finished working

with it, add 1 tablespoon water and return it to low heat until it has softened enough to work.

This glaze is sometimes used on the tops of éclairs and puffs. It is necessary to glaze the small puffs (profiteroles) when assembling Gâteau Saint-Honoré or croquembouche.

Strawberry Sauce

makes 1½ cups

1 pint strawberries
½ cup confectioners' sugar
1 teaspoon lemon juice

1 egg white
⅛ teaspoon salt

Wash, hull, and mash the strawberries. Add the confectioners' sugar and the lemon juice. Beat the egg white with the

salt until stiff. Combine the egg white with the strawberry mixture and whip the sauce until light.

Mocha Sauce

makes 1¼ cups

12 ounces chocolate chips
6 tablespoons prepared extra strong coffee, hot

1 tablespoon vanilla extract

Combine all the ingredients in a food processor or blender. To thin the sauce, if necessary, beat in 1 or 2 tablespoons of

boiling water. This sauce can be covered and stored in the refrigerator. Reheat in a double boiler.

Chocolate Sauce I

makes 1¾ cups

1½ cups granulated sugar
1 cup water

1½ cups unsweetened cocoa powder

In a large heavy-bottomed pan, stir the sugar with the water to dissolve the sugar. Bring to a rolling boil without stirring and let boil for 2 minutes. Remove from the heat and beat in the cocoa, beating rapidly with a whisk. Beat until the sauce is thick and shiny. If too thick, it can be thinned with water or a little cream. Can be reheated.

Chocolate Sauce II

makes 1 cup

4 ounces (4 squares) unsweetened chocolate

1 cup brown sugar
½ cup cream

In a small pan or bowl set over hot water, melt the chocolate. Add the brown sugar and cream and stir constantly until sauce is thick. Do not let mixture come to a boil. Cream will curdle at high temperatures.

Lemon Sauce

makes 1½ cups

3 tablespoons unsalted butter
¾ cup sifted confectioners' sugar
3 egg yolks, or 2 whole eggs

½ cup boiling water
1 teaspoon grated lemon rind
2 to 3 tablespoons lemon juice

In the top pan of a double boiler over hot water, soften the butter and add the sugar; blend until creamy. Add the eggs. Slowly stir in the boiling water and cook until thick. Add the lemon rind and juice.

Butterscotch Sauce

makes 2 cups

1 cup firmly packed dark brown sugar
1 cup maple syrup or corn syrup

8 tablespoons unsalted butter
½ teaspoon salt
2 teaspoons vanilla extract
¾ cup cream, preferably light

Combine the brown sugar and syrup in a heavy pan over low heat and stir constantly until the sugar is completely dissolved. Raise heat and boil the mixture for 5 minutes. Remove from heat and add, without stirring, the butter, salt and vanilla. Let the mixture stand for about 5 minutes, then add the cream. Beat until the sauce is creamy and well blended. Keep warm over hot water.

Gâteau Paris-Brest

one 9-inch ring, 8 portions

2   batches of Pâte à Choux
1   egg
2   cups plus 1 tablespoon
    heavy cream
3   ounces sliced almonds

2   tablespoons granulated
    sugar
2   teaspoons vanilla extract
2   tablespoons confectioners'
    sugar

Line a baking sheet with parchment paper or wax paper, and trace a 9-inch circle on it. Or you can butter and flour the baking sheet; knock off excess flour and mark a 9-inch circle with the inverted rim of a cake pan. Fit a pastry bag with a plain round #9 tube, ¾-inch opening.

Prepare the 2 batches of chou paste, but do not combine them. Fill a pastry bag with one batch of the paste and carefully pipe a ring inside the marked line. Pipe a second ring inside the first one and touching it, refilling the pastry bag when necessary. Pipe a third ring on top of the lower two. Gently smooth the shape with a spatula.

Preheat oven to 425°F. Place the oven rack at the middle level. Beat the egg with 1 tablespoon of the heavy cream, and brush the mixture over the ring. Sprinkle with the sliced almonds.

Set the baking sheet on the middle level in the preheated oven and bake for 20 minutes. Lower heat to 375°F and bake for an additional 20 minutes. Turn off the oven and

remove the baking sheet. Pierce the sides of the ring every 2 inches to release the steam. Return the sheet to the turned-off oven. Close the oven door. After 5 minutes with the door closed, open the door and prop it open slightly. Allow the ring to cool for an additional 30 minutes. Remove to a rack to cool completely.

With a large serrated knife, such as a bread knife, slice the ring horizontally into halves with small sawing motions. If there is any moist dough in the center, scrape it out with a fork or spoon.

Just before serving whip the 2 cups cream and flavor it with the 2 tablespoons granulated sugar and the vanilla. Spread the lower half of the ring with the flavored whipped cream. Or pipe the cream in swirls with a #9 star tip tube. Set the upper half of the ring lightly on the cream-filled base and sprinkle confectioners' sugar through a strainer to cover the top.

Variation: Add ½ cup praline powder to the whipped cream. The ring can also be filled with 3 cups Crème Pâtissière (see Index).

Beignets with Quick Apricot Sauce

makes about 50

Prepare a batch of Pâte à Choux, and add to it 2 teaspoons grated orange rind.

Heat about 1 inch of oil in a skillet or fryer to 360°F. Using 2 teaspoons, drop heaping spoons of the dough into the oil. Fry a few beignets at a time, for about 5 minutes, until they are crisp and golden brown. Drain on paper towels and keep warm while you continue with the frying.

Sift ¼ cup confectioners' sugar and sprinkle on the beignets. Serve with apricot sauce spooned over them.

Quick Apricot Sauce

1 cup apricot preserves
¼ cup water

2 tablespoons Cognac,
  Kirsch or orange liqueur
  (optional)

Place the preserves and water in a saucepan over moderate heat and beat until blended. Put the sauce through a strainer and return it to the pan. Add the liqueur if you use it and serve the sauce hot. Makes about 1 cup.

Profiteroles au Chocolat

makes 48 tiny puffs, 8 portions

1 batch Pâte à Choux
1 egg yolk
1 teaspoon cold water

Filling

1 pint vanilla ice cream, or 1 cup heavy cream flavored with 2 tablespoons sugar and 1 teaspoon vanilla extract

Sauce

2 ounces (2 squares) unsweetened chocolate
1 tablespoon unsalted butter
⅓ cup boiling water
1 cup sugar

Prepare the *pâte à choux*. Prepare 2 baking sheets: line them with foil or parchment paper; or butter and flour the baking sheets and shake off excess flour. Adjust the oven racks, one above center level and the other below, and preheat oven to 425°F for at least 10 minutes.

Fit a pastry bag with a #3 or #4 plain round tube (¼ inch or less), and pipe out 1-inch rounds, allowing 2 inches between them. Or drop batter by teaspoons. Beat egg yolk and water together and brush the wash on the tops of the profiteroles.

Bake at 425°F for 15 minutes; lower the heat to 375°F and bake for 5 minutes more. Turn off the oven, pierce the puffs with the tip of a knife or skewer, and let them stay in the turned-off oven for about 10 minutes. Remove puffs and let them cool completely before filling.

Allow the ice cream to soften very slightly. Split the puffs and put about 1 teaspoon of ice cream on the bottom halves. With a spoon, or your finger, round the ice cream into a ball, cover with the top of the puff, and place in the freezer. If puffs are not to be used that day, wrap them, when they are frozen solid, first in plastic, then in foil. They will keep for several weeks.

If using whipped cream, whip the cream with the sugar and vanilla and fill the puffs as described.

Make the sauce: In the top pan of a double boiler, or a small pan set over hot water, melt the chocolate and butter together. When completely melted, add ⅓ cup boiling water and blend well. Add 1 cup sugar. Boil the sauce over direct heat without stirring for about 5 minutes.

When the sauce is cold it is very thick. It can be reheated over boiling water.

Place the filled profiteroles on a serving platter, dribble a tiny amount of sauce over them and serve the rest of the sauce in a bowl or pitcher. Or you can mound 6 profiteroles on each of 8 dessert plates and pour the sauce over them before serving.

Variations: See the section on sauces for other ideas.

Croquembouche

10 portions

35 to 40 small cream puff shells (profiteroles)	Caramel Glaze (see Index)
1½ cups Crème Pâtissière (see Index), or sweetened whipped cream	20 crystallized violets (optional)

About 1 hour before serving, fill the puffs with *crème pâtissière* (pastry cream) or with whipped cream. Make the caramel glaze and keep it warm while constructing the pyramid. Dip the little puffs, one at a time, into the caramel and form a 9-inch circle with the puffs on a flat plate or a pedestal dish. Place a smaller circle of caramel-dipped puffs on top of the first circle, and continue forming smaller circles until you have formed a pyramid, ending with a single puff on top.

Cool the caramel to room temperature. Dip a fork into the cooled syrup and slowly drizzle syrup around the stacked puffs to spin threads of sugar to resemble angel hair. Decorate the pyramid with crystallized violets and serve within an hour.

Gâteau Saint-Honoré

This classic dessert is named after St. Honoré, the patron saint of bakers and pastry chefs. St. Honoré was supposedly a medieval French Bishop named Honorius.

The cake consists of a flat disk of pâte sucrée (sweet pastry) which is topped with a ring of chou pastry and crowned with small puffs (profiteroles) which have been dipped into caramel glaze. The center is filled with almond pastry cream and topped with sliced almonds.

9-inch cake, 8 portions

	pâte sucrée for a 9-inch round (see Volume 2 index)
1	batch of Pâte à Choux
1	egg

1	teaspoon water
	Caramel Glaze (see Index)
2½	cups Almond Cream Filling (see Index)
3	ounces sliced almonds

Prepare 2 large baking sheets, nonstick or lined with foil. Make the *pâte sucrée* and roll it out 3/16 inch thick. Using a cake pan, plate or bowl, cut a 9-inch circle. Roll the circle of dough on your rolling pin and unroll on the prepared baking sheet. Prick all over with a fork or pastry pricker. Refrigerate the dough circle until ready to bake it.

Prepare the chou pastry. Using the same pan or plate you used to cut the pastry round, dip the edge into flour and then touch the edge to the second baking sheet to mark a circle for the chou pastry ring. Fit a pastry bag with a #9 plain round tube and fill the bag with the chou pastry. Pipe a circle inside the marked ring on the baking sheet.

Using the pastry bag, pipe out about 22 tiny puffs, 1¼ inches in diameter, allowing an inch between them. They can be piped inside and outside the chou pastry ring and, if necessary, on the other sheet containing the pastry circle.

Preheat oven to 425°F. Combine the egg with 1 teaspoon water to make egg wash and brush on the chou pastry ring and the puffs. Place the oven racks one above center level and the other below center. Butter the outside bottom of a 9-inch cake pan and place it on top of the pastry circle to keep it from rising during baking.

Bake the circle and the chou pastry ring and puffs for about 20 minutes. Remove the pastry circle and continue baking the ring and puffs for about 10 minutes longer. Reduce oven heat to 350°F and bake ring and puffs for an additional 5 minutes, or until crisp. Turn oven off, leave the door closed, and let puffs and ring dry out for about 10 minutes. Leave the door partly open and let them dry for 10 to 15 minutes more. Remove to a rack to cool.

While the pastry is baking, prepare the caramel glaze, which will be used to hold the cake together, and the almond cream filling. If the caramel glaze should set before you have finished working with it, add 1 tablespoon water and return it to low heat until it has softened enough to work.

Place the pastry circle on a serving plate and place a

small ribbon of caramel around the rim to hold the chou ring in place. Using a fork, dip the puffs into the caramel. Use a second fork to arrange them next to each other on the puff ring. Dribble caramel on the tops of the puffs.

Fill the center of the ring with almond cream filling, and sprinkle sliced almonds on the top of the filling.
Variations: The ring may be filled with sweetened whipped cream and fresh strawberries or raspberries, ice cream or sherbets.

Craggy Strawberry Puffs

makes 8 to 10 large puffs

1   batch Pâte à Choux (see index)
1   recipe sweetened whipped cream or other filling (see index)

1   pint strawberries, sliced confectioners' sugar

These use a different baking technique. Do not use a pastry bag, but drop heaping tablespoons of dough onto a lined baking sheet, leaving 2 inches of space between them. Do not smooth them down; you want jagged tops. Cover the puffs with an inverted roasting pan, which must be smaller than the baking sheet.

Bake the puffs in a preheated 425°F oven for 20 minutes. Reduce heat to 375°F and bake for an additional 10 minutes. Remove the roasting pan from the baking sheet.

Pierce the puffs with a skewer or knife tip and leave in the turned-off oven with the door closed for 5 minutes. Open door slightly and leave for 10 minutes more. Remove to a rack to cool.

Split the cooled shells and fill with any of the cream fillings or sweetened whipped cream. Top with sliced strawberries. Replace the top half of the puff and sprinkle with confectioners' sugar. Serve at once.

100

Lemon Cream Puffs

makes 8 to 10 large puffsmakes 8 to 10 large puffs

½   cup water
4   tablespoons unsalted
     butter
     pinch of salt
1   teaspoon sugar
½   cup sifted all-purpose flour
2   large eggs

Egg Wash

1   egg
1   teaspoon water

Lemon Cream

½   cup heavy cream
½   cup Lemon Curd (recipe follows)
½   cup Crème Fraîche (recipe follows)
     grated rind of 1 lemon
1   tablespoon lemon juice
½   teaspoon lemon extract
     confectioners' sugar for
     tops of filled puffs

Following the method for *pâte à choux,* boil the water, butter, salt and sugar. Add flour all at once and beat vigorously. When mixture forms a ball and starts to film the bottom of the pan, beat in eggs, one by one, off the heat.

Line 2 baking sheets with foil or parchment paper. Preheat oven to 425°F. Fit a pastry bag with a #9 plain round tube (¾ inch) and pipe 2-inch rounds onto the sheets, allowing a generous 2 inches between the mounds.

Make the egg wash: Beat the egg with the water and brush the mixture on the tops of the puffs. Do not let the egg wash drip down the sides. Smooth down any little peaks that stand up.

Bake in the 425°F oven for 15 minutes. Lower the oven temperature to 375°F and bake for about 10 minutes more. When done, quickly pierce each puff to release steam and return the sheets to the turned-off oven. Leave them in the oven with the door ajar for 10 to 15 minutes.

Make the lemon cream: Whip the heavy cream until stiff, then beat in the lemon curd and all other ingredients.

When puffs are completely cool, split them and fill with lemon cream. Dust tops with confectioners' sugar.

Lemon Curd

makes about 2 cups

     grated rind of 2 lemons
⅔   cup sugar
5   large egg yolks

½   cup lemon juice (from 2 or
     3 lemons)
8   tablespoons unsalted
     butter, melted

Combine lemon rind and sugar. Beat in the egg yolks and lemon juice; blend well. Beat in the melted butter. Transfer to the top pan of a double boiler over hot water. Cook slowly, stirring constantly, until thick. Cool and store in a covered jar in the refrigerator. Keeps for 2 to 3 months.

Processor Method

Combine lemon rind, not grated, and the sugar and process until rind is ground fine. Add egg yolks and lemon juice and blend for 5 seconds. With machine running, pour melted butter through feed tube. Transfer to a double boiler to cook.

Crème Fraîche

makes about 2 cups

2   cups heavy cream

5   tablespoons buttermilk

True *crème fraîche* is French rich heavy cream, with a slightly acidic taste. It is widely used in France and is becoming more readily available in specialty shops across this country. It is fairly expensive, but it is easy to make a substitute at home.

Combine 2 cups heavy cream with 5 teaspoons buttermilk in a bowl or large jar. Stir well, cover tightly, and let stand at room temperature for at least 12 hours, perhaps for 24 hours if the room is cool. The cream will thicken.

Refrigerate for 24 hours before using. The cream can be kept under refrigeration for a month.

Apple Beignets with Apricot Sauce

4 portions

1	cup dried apricots
½	cup water
1	cinnamon stick
	juice of ½ lemon
2	batches Pâte à Choux
1	small cooking apple

¼	teaspoon grated lemon rind
1	tablespoon brown sugar
	oil for frying
	granulated sugar

Make the apricot sauce: Start the day before by soaking the dried apricots in water to cover overnight. Next day drain apricots and place in a saucepan with ½ cup water, the cinnamon stick and lemon juice. Simmer gently for about 15 minutes, until apricots are very tender. Purée through a food mill or in a blender. Keep the sauce warm.

Make the chou paste. Peel, core, and grate the apple. Stir apple bits into the dough with the lemon rind and brown sugar.

Heat oil in a deep-fryer to 350°F, or until a cube of bread browns in 40 seconds. Drop heaped teaspoons of the dough into the hot oil. Fry only a few beignets at a time for 5 to 7 minutes, until golden. Drain beignets on paper towels and keep hot until all of them have been fried.

Sprinkle granulated sugar over the beignets and serve them with the apricot sauce.

Variation: For banana beignets, add 1 mashed ripe banana to the chou paste; add 1 tablespoon brown sugar and a pinch of pumpkin pie spice. Sprinkle beignets with chopped nuts before frying them.

Part Five

CLASSIC ITALIAN SUPPER

With pasta and other Italian foods so popular in America, you may want to consider a dinner party with foods redolent of the flavors of Italy. This menu can be served summer or winter. Although the recipes here are planned to serve 4 persons, they can be doubled or even quadrupled if you plan a larger gathering.

Linguine with fresh tomato sauce is the first course, to be served at room temperature. Pork loin cooked in milk and accompanied by zucchini simmered with onions is the main course. Now that American pork is leaner than ever and contains only slightly more calories than beef (3 ounces of cooked pork provides 198 calories; a similar serving of beef provides 192) and is one of the greatest single dietary sources of thiamine, a B vitamin, we feel that pork is a meat for all seasons. On a sweltering summer evening the meat can be served slightly chilled. Hot, crusty Italian bread spread with Casino Butter—a butter mixed with herbs, pepper and pimiento—is our bread accompaniment. Dessert puffs made with chou paste and bursting with a sweet ricotta cheese filling, similar to a cannoli filling, is our dessert. For a finale serve a rich brewed regular or decaffeinated coffee. For an additional Italian touch, serve thimbles of Sambuca, the Roman liqueur, into which you have dropped a coffee bean or two, the way they serve it on the Piazza di Spagna.

Red, green and white are the colors of the Italian flag. What about a centerpiece of flaming red zinnias, green privet and white snapdragons? Or a basket overflowing with fresh fruit.

If it is tomato time and your garden is overflowing with the small Italian plum tomatoes, you might want to dry some. In southern Italy the tomatoes are spread on wicker trays and dried on rooftops, or strung in bunches and hung outside to dry naturally. Unfortunately, dried Italian tomatoes are expensive and sometimes hard to come by, so here is a recipe for making your own:

Halve Italian plum tomatoes lengthwise and lay them cut sides up on an oiled baking sheet. Place the sheet in a very low oven, about 150°F, and check every few hours to make sure tomatoes are not burning. They should be drying out, slowly. The tomatoes should shrink to one third of their original size when done; this could take 10 to 12 hours. Pack the tomatoes into clean Mason jars, pouring olive or vegetable oil over each layer of tomatoes. Cover the last layer of tomatoes with about 2 inches of oil. Cover and refrigerate the tomatoes. Since the oil acts as a seal to prevent air from touching the tomatoes (air allows mold to form), it is essential that no bits of tomato stick up through the oil. The tomatoes keep for about 6 months, refrigerated, but they are so delicious in salads, pasta dishes, rice dishes, stews and soups, so they will probably be long gone before then.

Italian Wines

Americans drink more Italian *vino* than any other imported wine. The reasons are obvious; the wine is light, refreshing and low-priced. Soave, a dry white wine, is the most popular of these imports. While it has been criticized as having little character, it is nevertheless a pleasant addition to a meal of fish or poultry.

Italy produces an astonishing variety of red and white wines at competitive prices, as well as a number of exceptional offerings equal to the best from France, Germany and America. There are the familiar red wines such as Bardolino, a light dry wine from Verona; the mellow Valpolicella, also from the same area; Barbaresco, flinty and full-bodied; and Barolo, another full-bodied red wine perfectly suited for pasta with red sauce. While most Chianti no longer comes in the distinctive, straw-wrapped bottle, it is one of the best full-bodied red wines available. Fruity Orvieto, mellow Soave, very dry Verdicchio, and light, dry Frascati are four of Italy's most famous and popular white wines.

A rich Barolo in winter, a lighter Bardolino in the summer, or a Chianti Classico anytime would be an appropriate choice for the pork roast and the zucchini. If you prefer a white wine, a Verdicchio or Soave is equally acceptable with this classic Italian meal.

CLASSIC ITALIAN SUPPER FOR FOUR

Linguine with Fresh Tomato Sauce

Pork Loin Cooked in Milk

Zucchini and Onion Sauté

Italian Bread with Casino Butter

Cream Puffs with Sweet Ricotta Filling

Wine Suggestion: Chianti Classico

MARKET LIST

Meat

2½   pounds pork loin roast

Fruit and Vegetables

6 large tomatoes	1 bunch watercress
1 large sweet onion	6 small zucchini
5 medium onions	1 green pepper
1 head garlic	1 shallot
1 carrot	1 lemon
1 bunch parsley	1 orange
1 bunch fresh basil	

linguine
olive oil
red-wine vinegar
sun-dried tomatoes
pimientos
flour
butter
fennel seeds
milk
orégano

Staples

Worcestershire sauce
eggs
almond extract
ricotta cheese
heavy cream
sugar
candied fruit
chocolate bits
brandy

Linguine with Fresh Tomato Sauce

4 generous portions

1 pound linguine, preferably imported	¾ cup olive oil
salt	⅓ cup red-wine vinegar
6 large red-ripe tomatoes	freshly ground black pepper
1 large sweet onion	½ cup chopped sun-dried tomatoes, or ½ cup chopped pimientos
2 garlic cloves	
½ cup chopped fresh parsley	
½ cup chopped fresh basil	

Cook linguine in 6 quarts boiling water with 2 tablespoons salt until tender but very firm. Drain and reserve in a basin of cold water.

Blanch the fresh tomatoes in boiling water for 1 minute, until skins start to pucker. Drain, and peel off skins. Chop tomatoes and drain them; reserve the liquid for another use. Peel the onion and cut into paper-thin slices; there should be about 2 cups. Peel and mince the garlic. Combine chopped fresh tomatoes with remaining sauce ingredients and mix well. Taste for seasoning; add up to 2 teaspoons salt and pepper as needed.

Drain linguine well and toss with tomato sauce. Cover and leave at room temperature for several hours, or refrigerate overnight. Toss again just before serving.

Pork Loin Cooked in Milk

4 portions

2	garlic cloves		1	tablespoon oil
1	medium-size onion		1	tablespoon butter
1	carrot		2½	to 3 cups milk
1	tablespoon fennel seeds		1	teaspoon salt
2½	pounds pork loin, tied with string			freshly ground black pepper
3	tablespoons flour			watercress
				orange slices

Peel garlic cloves and cut into thin slivers. Peel and chop onion. Scrape and chop carrot. Crush fennel seeds in a mortar with a pestle. With the tip of a small knife, make incisions in the pork and insert the slivers of garlic. Dust the pork with flour. Heat the oil and butter in a heavy pot and brown the pork well on all sides. While the meat is browning, heat the milk to just under a simmer; do not let it boil. Sprinkle the browned pork with onion, carrot and fennel, and add the salt and pepper to taste. Pour in 2½ cups of the hot milk. Simmer the meat, covered, over very low heat for 1½ hours, turning it once. Uncover and add more hot milk if necessary. Simmer for 30 minutes longer, until the sauce turns golden and thick.

Remove the pork to a carving board and let it cool for 30 minutes. Slice the meat and arrange on a serving platter with watercress and orange slices as a garnish. The milky sauce will be slightly clotted, if desired, purée in a blender or food processor, reheat and pour it over the meat.

Zucchini and Onion Sauté

4 portions

6	small zucchini, about 2 pounds altogether
3	medium-size onions
2	garlic cloves
½	cup olive oil

½	teaspoon salt
	freshly ground black pepper
1	tablespoon chopped parsley

Gently scrub zucchini to remove grit, trim stem and blossom ends, and cut the vegetables into 1-inch cubes. Peel and chop the onions. Peel and mince the garlic. Combine zucchini and onions in a heavy skillet. Pour in the olive oil and add the salt, pepper to taste, and the minced garlic. Cover and simmer gently for 15 minutes, turning occasionally. Remove cover during the last 5 minutes to allow excess moisture to evaporate. Garnish with chopped parsley.

Italian Bread with Casino Butter

4 portions, or more

1	large loaf of Italian bread
	Casino Butter
8	ounces salted butter
¼	green bell pepper
¼	red bell pepper or pimiento
1	shallot
1	tablespoon chopped parsley

¼	teaspoon crumbled dried orégano
	juice of ½ lemon
1	tablespoon Worcestershire sauce
	freshly ground black pepper

Make the Casino butter: Let the butter soften at room temperature. Trim and mince the green and red peppers; if using a pimiento, rinse it to get rid of seeds. Peel and mince the shallots. Combine softened butter with the vegetables, herbs, lemon juice, Worcestershire sauce and about 10 grinds of black pepper. Mix well. Chill the butter slightly.

Cut the bread into thick slices, leaving the slices attached at the bottom of the loaves. Spread casino butter on both sides of the slices. Partially wrap the loaf in foil, place on a baking sheet and heat in a 350°F oven for 10 minutes. Reserve any remaining butter in the refrigerator.

Cream Puffs with Sweet Ricotta Filling

12 to 14 puffs

1 batch of Pâte à Choux	2 tablespoons brandy
¼ teaspoon almond extract	1 cup heavy cream
	¼ cup sugar
Ricotta Filling	¼ cup chopped chocolate bits
2 cups ricotta cheese	
¼ cup candied fruits	

Make the dough, beating in the almond extract after the last egg has been added. Shape large cream puffs: drop the dough by tablespoon on a well-greased and floured baking sheet, dropping the mounds far apart. Bake in a preheated 425°F oven for 10 minutes, then reduce oven heat to 375°F and bake for 25 minutes longer. Cool thoroughly, then split and spoon in the filling.

To make the filling: Drain the cheese well. Chop the candied fruits and soak them in the brandy. Whip the cream until stiff and combine with the cheese. Gently fold in the sugar, fruits and any remaining brandy, and chocolate bits. Makes about 4 cups filling.

INDEX